ONE LIGHT

An Owner's Manual for the Human Being

ONE LIGHT

An Owner's Manual for the Human Being

Mitchell Gilbert

with an introduction by

His Holiness
M. R. Bawa Muhaiyaddeen
...May the Joy of God ever surround him

ONE LIGHT PRESS
Merion Station, Pennsylvania

Library of Congress Control Number: 2005931036

ISBN-13: 978-0-9771267-0-5
ISBN-10: 0-9771267-0-6

Merion Station, Pennsylvania 19066

First published in 1980
Samuel Weiser, Inc.
740 Broadway
New York, NY 10003

Third printing 2005
One Light Press

Bismillahirrahmanirraheem

In the Name of that

GOD

Who rules over
everything
with absolute mercy
and compassion

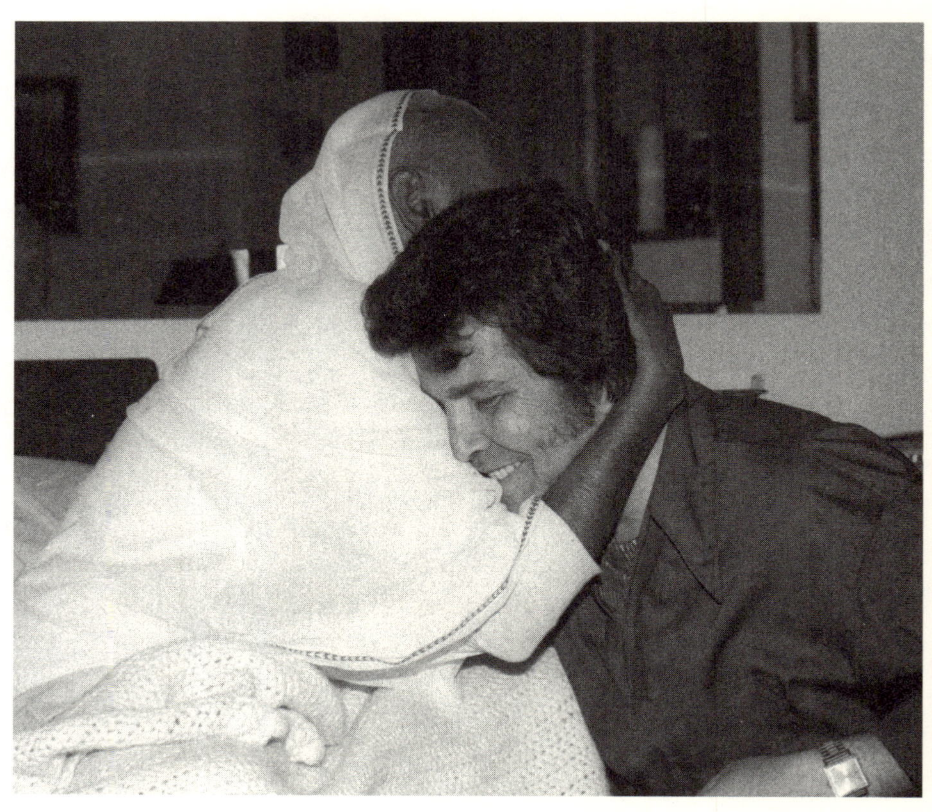

DEDICATION

To Sheikh M. R. Bawa Muhaiyaddeen, a supreme example of those who receive revelation and inspire generations of good people to pursue wisdom.

And to my son, Darrell, who writes songs of encouragement and praise of God for those on this path.

CONTENTS

ACKNOWLEDGEMENT

SUPPOSE A DAM WERE built across a river. Then suppose a passageway were opened to allow some of the river water to pass through the dam. Could the dam take credit for the water that passed through it?

It is with that same understanding that I realize that the words in this book are not mine. I cannot claim them as my own. As will be seen by the reader as he studies this book, our bodies, our minds and our desires are like a dam holding back the river of Truth. Our conditioned responses and our attachments are the cement that binds together the rocks that hold back the Truth.

There is a passageway in each inner heart that can be opened up to allow that Truth to pass through. It exists as a potential within each human being. But it is no easy thing to discover that passageway. It is more difficult, still, to open it and allow God's Truth to come through.

We need a very special kind of teacher to show us the secret passageway within our hearts. The teacher must know, fully, the nature of dams and be able to detect the strengths and weaknesses of each particular dam. He must understand the nature of the river and what its properties

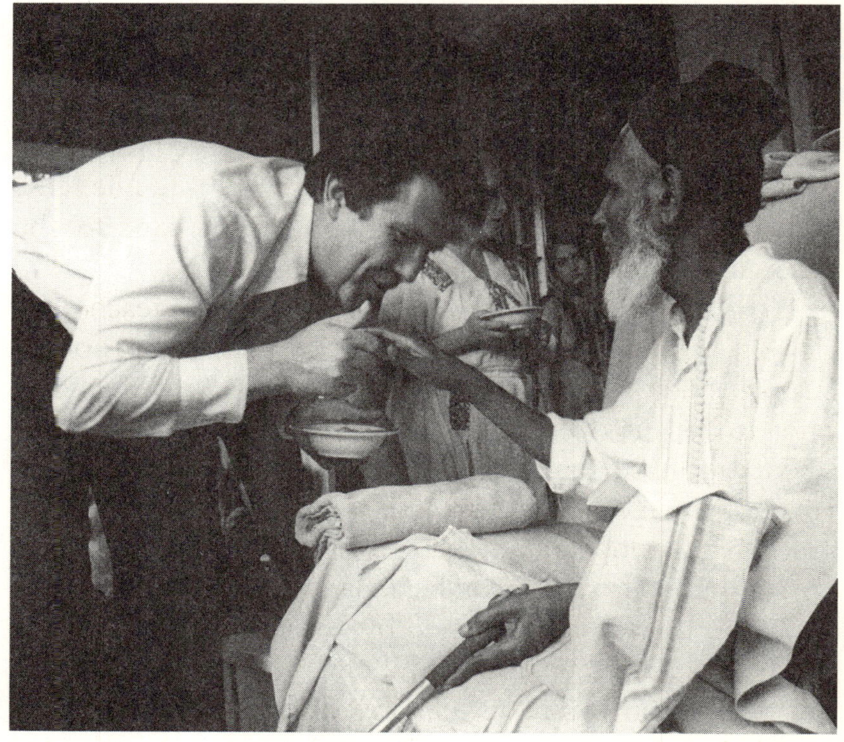

We need a very special kind of teacher to show us the secret passageway within our hearts.

are Then he must be able to convey all that he knows to the student and he must be able to overcome the student's fear or resistance by being that river of Truth in his every example.

Sadly, such teachers are very rare. In this era, when the stresses caused by rapid change and rampant destruction have impelled so many to seek, with growing intensity, that inner Truth, there has been an equivalent increase in the merchandising of solutions. This is not to say that there is no

Truth in the formulas being sold by the purveyors of new religions, psychotherapies and mystical techniques. On the other hand, the fact that there are potatoes in potato chips does not make such snacks nourishing food.

If we knew how and were willing to farm for our food, we would not be the victims of those with a proprietary interest in selling us their particular brand of adulterated and packaged food. Similarly, we must learn to farm for the Truth inherent within our own lives.

Thus, I owe a particular debt of gratitude to a teacher we call Bawa Muhaiyaddeen. He is one who teaches people to farm. Though he is extremely old, little is known of him prior to his discovery in the forests of northern Sri Lanka (then called Ceylon) about 40 years ago by a family of Hindus. When he began to teach them how to farm for the Truth, he developed a following that called him Guru Bawa. Later, Muslims from the southern part of the island heard of him. They also were impressed by his approach to teaching the Truth, and they began to call him Sheikh. Still later, one of these students came to the United States, and seeing the popularity of some he considered charlatans, he pleaded with Bawa to visit this country. In October, 1971, when another of Bawa's students came to the United States as a representative from Sri Lanka to a World Health Organization conclave being held here, Bawa came with him. He has been dividing his time between the two countries since then. Due to the Christian culture of many American students, the title Guru and the title Sheikh were rejected and they began calling him His Holiness, Bawa Muhaiyaddeen.

Bawa, himself, eschews all such titles. Only our appreciation of him compels us to set him apart in some manner, and reference to his genuine holiness seems as apt a way as any. It is my personal belief that without his guidance, this writer would not have discovered the potential within the heart of a human being and this heart would not have opened—in which case there would be no book.

Yet, Bawa Muhaiyaddeen constantly reminds us that all praise belongs only to God. So, while Bawa's name is mentioned several times throughout the book, it is with full knowledge that without God there would be no river of Truth; and without Truth, a book is only scribbles on a page.

1980

Introduction by His Holiness M. R. Bawa Muhaiyaddeen

May God protect, bless and cherish those in this world who have Love and Faith. May God bless His representatives, His messengers and all those who become True Human Beings, for they are perfection among all of God's creations.

God is the Perfection intermingled with life. Man experiences the Plenitude of that Perfection when he sees the Effulgence of Love in his heart, when he hears the explanation of Purity within his heart, when his heart resonates with the Justice based on integrity, and when, as a result, he knows the Serenity and Peacefulness of the heart that is open to True Wisdom.

God alone can provide that True Wisdom that gives Clarity to men's thoughts. That True Wisdom supports the Human Being, fills his own wisdom with Love and brings Peace and Serenity to the Perfect Purity of his heart. God bestows that Wisdom as the basic foundation and support for man's life.

God also is the Grace within that True Wisdom that He has given only to mankind. He exists as the Light within that Grace, the Plenitude within that Light, the Perfection of that

M.R. BAWA MUHAIYADDEEN,
May Allah be pleased with him

Plenitude, the Resplendence, as Himself within that Effulgence—and, as a Power within Himself—He exists as the Qualities and Actions and all the potential that exists within the Wisdom, Serenity and Peacefulness that He has provided.

Those who have Love and Faith must think a little. For more than 200 million years, so many species and races have appeared and reappeared. Various ideas, philosophies and religions have appeared, changed and reappeared over and over again. The world has seen many different kinds of books, many kinds of research, many kinds of art, many kinds of sexual acts, many kinds of magic, many mantras, festivals, dances, songs, awards and titles. The world has seen philosophy books, religious doctrines, the Bible, the Koran and other testaments. We have seen scientific investigations, investigations into psychic phenomena, investigations into history, into mind energies, into horoscopes, into yoga and into various ways to achieve peace, all published in book form. People read such books and derive meaning from them based on the individual's level of wisdom. People read religious texts, the puranas, the Koran, the Bible and other testaments, and by the knowledge acquired from those books, they carry out the rituals prescribed in each. They soak themselves in their rituals and keep crawling onwards.

But God is the Causal Being, the Creator without form of any kind; without body, shape, color or shade; without fame or honors; without a name, place, beginning or end. He is such an All-Pervasive Omnipresence that He cannot be described by comparison with any form or all form. It is His Grace that manifests as True Wisdom within the Human Being. That Wisdom of Grace, that Divine Wisdom, cannot be comprehended by what we normally think of as intelligence. Yet it stands resonating within man's heart, giving explanations constantly.

As that Wisdom of Grace blossoms within man's heart, it

forms the flower garden where God's Power can reside. It is there that the Truth can resonate from that Power; the steadfast Determination of absolute Faith can emerge from that Truth; the Resplendent Light can shine forth from that Determined Faith; the fullness of Plenitude can manifest from that Light; the Perfect Divine Luminous Wisdom of God's Effulgence can shine forth from that Plenitude; and the Power of Truth that is God is within that Divine Luminous Wisdom. God has deposited this entire explanation within man's inner heart.

That heart is an ocean of Wisdom. There is nothing that can compare with that Wisdom. It is a vast ocean of Grace. It is God's Power.

It is with this Wisdom of Grace that man has to see both what is within and what is outside. With this Wisdom of Grace, he can see the world of the Soul (the Original Effulgence of God's creation), the world of hell (this world of form) and the heavenly world (the Light of Truth).

God reposes within this flower garden called the heart—within this ocean of Wisdom—and provides the explanations that enables us to see each and every thing through the Wisdom within wisdom, the Eternal, All-pervasive, Omnipresent Effulgence.

My beloved children, gems of my eyes, not until you have learned this Wisdom, not until you have searched for and found this Wisdom, not until you have reached the state in which you see everything through the Clarity of this Wisdom, can it be possible for you to know yourself, know your Soul, or know God—no matter how many books you may have read or how many investigations you may have conducted.

You cannot learn this by reading religious texts or philosophy books. You cannot achieve knowledge of it through some miracle, or magic, or by engaging in any of the arts, or through sensual pleasures. The Wisdom capable of knowing this Truth must arise within us as a basic principle. Books and other methods cannot make us understand this.

What can be learned through religions is just one small portion. Our personal experiences, philosophies, yoga techniques, each can teach only one tiny fraction. And the man who relies on sakti (energy), whether of the spirit, of sound, or the energy within the elements of the body or any of the 400 million, million and 10,000 spiritual saktis man creates, does not realize that he is turning spiritual yearning into petty miracles through these various energies—yet, he, himself, is the cause and the creator of all those energies on which he has come to rely. He projects the qualities of his own mind and creates saktis out of them. He becomes the guru or priest for the energies within his own physical elements and, like a god, he commands them to perform miraculous feats. Then, he worships that energy.

There are many different books, religions and techniques that teach how to use these energies to perform feats and tricks. Other books explain the use of other kinds of energy. There are millions of books on art, drama, psychology, sensual pleasure and sexual techniques. The world goes on studying these continually. People soak themselves in such thought until their hearts succumb to what they have learned. Then they go on dying and being born over and over again.

If, my precious children, my beloved children who are the gems of my eye, will only think a little, they will see that there is another book—a great big book—called man. Everything that exists in all of the universes also exists within man. All of the saktis or energies are subdued within man. Also within man is that True Wisdom that will enable him to transcend and stand beyond all these things. First, that Wisdom will conquer all the saktis and go beyond them; then understand all the seeming miracles and go beyond them; then see through all illusion; then conquer the mind; then overcome attachments to physical vision and the arts; and then, as that Wisdom of Grace that sees God as God, it will reveal the resonances and pulsations that explain Truth.

The cardinal rule must be, therefore, to study the method of learning the basic supports on which True Wisdom stands. That is Wisdom brought into action. That is the Wisdom of Grace, Wisdom of the Soul, Effulgent Wisdom. To do that, we must seek and acquire that state of Purity and Perfection that is capable of serving as a commander of a Realized Human Being's Divine Wisdom. That is the Wisdom of Grace.

Wisdom of Grace emerges from the Grace of God, resonates in His Grace, manifests, shines and resplends until the Realized Human Being's Wisdom is vaster than the vastest ocean. That is Divine Luminous Wisdom. The learned ones who understand this become the teachers of Divine Luminous Wisdom.

Every group may have its guru. But that guru may deal with a section that teaches religion only. Another guru may teach racial discrimination, another philosophy, and others may teach only magic or control of saktis or only devotion. There may be many individual sections.

But Divine Luminous Wisdom is something through which one can understand and know all of the universes. Divine Luminous Wisdom is the Wisdom through which God (in man) communicates with God as God within God, Grace within Grace—that Wisdom of Perfection and Plenitude that manifests as Wisdom within man and communes with God. This is Divine Luminous Wisdom.

When we look with this Wisdom, the whole world appears as a book. We are able to learn some small portion from each and everything we see. Trees, flowers, insects, the sun, moon and stars, birth, death, everything we see, hear, taste, touch or smell—all become the books from which we can learn. Each thing contains a story within itself. A person must dissect and analyze each story and discover whether it contains a clue to that path which leads to God. He must constantly analyze with his Wisdom to see which is the right path and which is wrong. Then he will see that the lives in the ocean, the lives on the earth, everything that moves and the things that do not move are all books that must be read.

The Divine Luminous Wisdom that has the capacity to read all these books is called Wisdom of Gnanam. And to understand the explanations of what one reads with Wisdom of Gnanam, the True Gnana Guru is needed. That Gnana Guru transcends all saktis, all religions, all caste differences and any need for miraculous feats, tricks, magics, meditations, philosophies or scriptures. He goes beyond all of them to merge in Oneness with that Primal One who stands beyond even the beyond of all religions and philosophies.

It is only one who has that Wisdom of Gnanam capable of knowing all of everything—the Wisdom vaster than the largest oceans—who will have that level of realization. If we succeed in finding such a Guru, the liberation of our Soul is assured on that very day.

My dear beloved children, instead of indulging in the world or in meditation, in the arts or in mantras, tantras and the like, if you can understand this Wisdom and its Power and the state of Gnanam, if you can seek that Wisdom, you will receive and learn truly valuable lessons. If you understand this, you will reach a state where you will understand the inner and outer meanings of all the secrets in the world.

Therefore, my fellow beings of Truth who have been born with me, even more than reading this book, if you seek to acquire that Treasure of Plenitude, that Treasure of God's Qualities and God's Explanations, that Resplendent Treasure—if you seek and acquire that Treasure called Wisdom, that alone will give you the fullness and the Perfection of Plenitude that cuts away the chain of birth and death. That will be the good state.

This book will talk of the steps you must take to understand the explanation of Wisdom. This book will help burnish the shrine of our Wisdom. It will help to clarify the explanations of Wisdom. It will explain the Truth of the Pulsations of our Luminous Wisdom and of the Brilliance of the Effulgence of our Soul.

This book is a signpost. Like a railway signal, it stands on the path of your journey, saying "Stop" or "Go." It is a helpmate for your Soul. It is a car that will give you a ride. It will be a map for your journey in your travels to and fro. This book will enable you to examine the true state of your actions as you might look something up in an almanac or check out something else by your horoscope.

If you reflect with your Wisdom as you read this book, you will find that it points out and explains to you what that Wisdom is, what the Soul is, what Gnanam is, what God is, what man is, and so many other things.

Therefore, my beloved children, gems of my eye, your research into Wisdom will show you that everything in this world is in the form of books or stories. And Wisdom is required in order to read all those stories. Wisdom is required to see that All-pervasive Reality that exists as the Wisdom within wisdom. Seek that Wisdom first and strive for it. Find the Qualities of that Wisdom. Find the actions of that Wisdom. Find the conduct of that Wisdom and its behavior.

Find the virtues of that Wisdom. Find the resonance of that Wisdom—its explanations and pulsations. Find the Power that reposes in the flower garden of your heart. Find that heart. If you succeed in acquiring the Wisdom that can find all of these, then you can utilize it to know all of everything.

We give you this book as a portion of those explanations; as the explanation of Wisdom. Please take these explanations of Wisdom into your understanding. Polish them with your heart and then analyze that Wisdom and look at it. You will find that you are analyzing yourself through that Wisdom. If you analyze yourself, you will be analyzing your Soul. If you succeed in analyzing the Soul, you will find it possible to analyze Grace. If you can analyze Grace, you can analyze God. If you can analyze God, you will be able to see His Power. This is the path of excellence.

Please take this book with love—this book on the research of Wisdom. Read it through your wisdom and learn the means to acquire Wisdom.

May God bless you with that Wisdom of Grace. Through that Wisdom, may He give you the explanations needed to know where He is and where you are. My children, while you read this book with the fullness of your heart, please think and reflect so that these explanations will shine forth from your heart. And with the Plenitude of that heart, and understanding the resonances emanating from that heart, you can merge as One with God. I pray to God that you will succeed in your efforts to reach Him. May God bless you all. Amen.

M. R. Bawa Muhaiyaddeen

ONE LIGHT

An Owner's Manual
for the Human Being

I
WHAT ARE WE SEEKING?

WHAT IS IT YOU WANT? What are you really looking for? Self-realization? God-realization? Perfection? Contentment? An end to depression, anger and anxiety? A little peace in your life? Love?

There is a built-in Wisdom—a radar system—that can lead you to all of these things. But first, your consciousness must rise above your five senses. Otherwise, how can you know anything other than what has already passed?

We must understand what the self is before we can pursue self-realization. Otherwise, what are we pursuing?

We must have a model by which to judge Perfection; otherwise, how can we correct ourselves?

We must know God in order to meditate, commune or merge with that Universal One. Otherwise, what are we worshiping?

Think of it this way: Which came first, the pen or the alphabet? Obviously, some scheme for communicating with written symbols first had to exist within someone's consciousness. Otherwise, of what use would a writing instrument be?

So many of us are like children holding pens but with no

knowledge of the alphabet. How can we write? That is why it so often happens that prayer, meditation, psychedelic drugs, encounter groups, sense-awareness training, positive thinking, macrobiotic diets, various yogas, philosophies, psychologies, religions, mantras, and thousands of other self-help, self-realization and God-realization methods and techniques fail to bring their adherents to ultimate Contentment and Peace.

If we know the alphabet, then the pen is useful. If we know God, then meditation is automatic. If we know what Perfection is, then we can correct ourselves. If we know where Contentment is, nothing can keep us from it.

It may take some of us a lifetime of searching before we realize that we really don't know what we are looking for. Sometimes the diligence with which we search can become such a cause for pride that it no longer matters to us whether we find anything. The search itself becomes enough. We become long-time members of this group of seekers or that, and that becomes our way of life. We then encourage others to join our way of life. Every method has its missionaries.

Those who are younger in age—the potential joiners or likely customers for all the competing missionaries—suffer most of all. Those who believe they have "found a way" are often numb to disturbing doubts. The so-called true believer can scribble away happily for years without realizing that he isn't writing. His method sedates him and he forgets the anguish he felt at the beginning of his search.

But the new seeker is plagued with doubts. He knows only his own discontent with any certainty. He knows his sorrow, his anxiety, his anger and frustration. He knows what he wants to leave behind. But he does not know, for sure, either where he wants to go or how to get there. Phrases like God-realization, human potential, psychic awareness, contentment and peace of mind all sound appealing. Yet, while still at the beginning of his search, he realizes he is only guessing at what such lofty phrases really mean. He knows what he doesn't know and that frightens him.

In a very real sense, this doubt-ridden, fearfully confused beginner is a lot closer to the Truth than his older brothers and sisters. He has not yet made the sometimes irreversible mistake of putting faith in the pen or in the method. He knows he still is scribbling. He is under no illusion that his scribbling is "the Way."

The sophisticated eclectic may be the most deluded of all. Too cynical to believe in any one "way" or method for achieving contentment, he creates an original recipe for living that includes bits and pieces from many of the various systems. He may practice some combination of tantric sex, hatha yoga, astrology, group faith healing, strict vegetarianism, and smoking a lot of marijuana. He may attend or even lead encounter groups, practice sensitivity training, participate in monthly full-moon ceremonies with an esoteric society or visit, at least once, every self-proclaimed guru that presents himself. Since the experienced eclectic often knows about more methods and techniques than the typical guru, such encounters usually prove fruitless.

But the teacher who serves only the Truth is not in business to sell a method or technique. He is not selling religion or pens. He knows your life is the only tool you need. His function is to reveal to you the true value and purpose of your life. Here, for example, is how one very experienced eclectic describes his first encounter with Bawa Muhaiyaddeen:

"When a young lady invited me to meet this 'Holy Man from Ceylon,' I didn't jump with excitement. That was in early January, 1972, and I told her, 'Look, I think a lot of us have become nothing more than guru groupies. There's nothing we need to know that hasn't been prerecorded right within our own being. No one outside us can tell us the Truth. We have to discover it for ourselves within our own lives.'

"As it turns out, I was telling her the truth. But I didn't realize then, how hopeless it is to try to discover that prerecorded Truth within your life if you really haven't discovered the nature of life. Fortunately for me, the young lady persisted and I agreed to go and meet Bawa Muhaiyaddeen.

"When we arrived at the run-down row-home in West Philadelphia where Bawa was staying on his first visit to America, we were invited up to a room on the second floor. There, several people were seated on the floor and Bawa was seated on a bed. In quick succession, I noticed his deep, penetrating eyes, his extreme age, his tiny, thin form and then—whap!—his incredibly loving gaze. I didn't know whether this person was holy or wise, but certainly he was loving.

"Immediately at ease with him, and warmed by his seemingly limitless Love for all who came into his presence, I decided to venture a few questions. A young exchange-student from Ceylon acted as interpreter. My questions were academic. It seems to me now that, for Bawa, the questions were on a par with asking, 'Who is buried in Grant's tomb?' Yet, they were the most profound mysteries I knew how to ask about at the time.

"His replies, however, always seemed to answer more than I had asked—as though, somehow, he understood the misunderstanding that caused me to ask that particular question. To say that his answers had the ring of Truth would be less than what actually occurred. It was as though, for the first time in my life, I realized that there was something akin to a tuning fork inside my heart. And just as striking a perfect 'A' on the piano will make the A-440 tuning fork ring out in sympathetic vibration, Bawa's words made this newly discovered tuning fork in my heart vibrate. It was a joyful experience.

"Of course I now recognize that the 'tuning fork' I experienced is a constant, built-in evaluator—an integral part of this instrument called life. Bawa was already teaching me about life on that very first visit. But at the time, all I realized was that it would be good to visit him again; so before I left, I asked for permission to return.

"During the next couple of weeks, I was there almost every night. Then, one evening, Bawa began giving an imitation of the ways people behave when they are high on grass. It seemed that he was showing me a movie of all my games. He imitated the way I laughed when I got high with male friends, the way I tried to seduce when I got high with a female, and the way in which I acted as though I had experienced revelations about God when I got high alone. Never once did he look at me; nevertheless, I took it all very personally.

"That night, I totally cleaned out all my secret caches of drugs. I gave away all my pipes, rolling papers and bags of grass. I went to sleep content. But by the next night, I was feeling incredibly depressed. I had been smoking grass fairly regularly for almost twenty years; two or three times a day for the past five years. Yet, for some reason, I didn't connect my depression with having just broken my smoking habit. All I knew was that I felt like crying and I didn't understand why. I decided to just go to sleep early and forget about it.

"At about 4 a.m. that morning I awoke with a dream that Bawa had come to me in my sleep and suggested that I eat a meal of rice, onions and parsley. I sat up in bed and thought, 'Now look, it is quite possible that a guru can come to you with some message in your sleep. But I can't imagine that he would come with a recipe for dinner.' So I just rolled over and went back to sleep. At about 6:30, my usual time for getting up, I had the very same dream again. It was as though someone were saying, 'Now don't forget: Rice, onions and parsley.'

"So on the way home from work that evening, I felt compelled to stop at a store and buy the required ingredients. Two friends were expected for dinner that evening, so I made a large quantity of rice, onions and parsley. One friend found the parsley bitter and kept removing it from her plate. I couldn't get enough of the parsley. I felt like a sponge just soaking it up. So I ate mine and hers.

"I felt better having eaten the meal and I greedily ate the left-overs the following evening. On that second evening, I felt so much better that I decided to ask Bawa about the dream. But before I could get my question out, the interpreter informed me that Bawa was saying something to me. 'You have been smoking ganja for nearly twenty years,' the interpreter translated. 'You had to give it up or your wisdom would never begin to grow.' Bawa smiled at me, showing me he wasn't judging me; merely stating a fact. 'But the residues are still in your blood stream,' Bawa continued. 'That is why you were experiencing such distress. The parsley is a blood cleanser. That is why I told you to eat the parsley.'

"Inexplicably, I began to cry. Here was a man who knew my illness even before I knew it and told me how to cure it. My mind raced through dozens of explanations for what had just taken place: The secret power of the Guru; the healing power of Love; the mystery of all life within God and God within all life; the Ineffable Oneness of everything. But while my mind raced, my heart understood something else intimately.

"For an entire lifetime, I had been holding on to what now seems like a nightmare. It was the feeling that I was hanging from some precipice by my fingertips. I wasn't conscious of any fear. I always believed that I could continue to hold on as long as necessary. I didn't even complain about the strain of such an ordeal. To me, it simply was what survival demanded.

"Now, suddenly, something deep within my heart was whispering to me, 'You can let go now. Nothing will happen to you. You can let go.'

"My God, how many times before that moment I had talked about letting go without any understanding of what it meant! It seemed that my entire life style, all that I preached and wrote about, the entire philosophy around which I had built my self-image, entailed letting go. But in that moment I saw that I had only let go of external manifestations. Inside, I had never let go of that absolute conviction that I was a separate individual and that I was the only one that I could ever trust. Survival depended on holding on to that self—that 'I'—that arrogance of the ego. What a lonely and deadly mistake!"

II
Who Are We Now?

"When 'I' am here, God is not.
When God is here, 'I' am not."

BAWA KEEPS SAYING that. What does it mean? If God is the Source of all life, shouldn't we be able to detect that Power of God within our lives? But when we examine our lives, which thing is God and which is "I"? Who am I? Who is God? What is the relationship between the two? Are there two, or is the sense of duality just an illusion? Is there really only the One? If so, what is this "I" that thinks there is more than one?

"When 'I' am here, God is not. When God is here, 'I' am not." What does Bawa mean by "here"? Certainly, if God is within all life—if He is the Power that provides life—He doesn't come and go. He must, by definition, be Omnipresent.

And there must be something that provides life. There has to be something inside the seed that causes it to grow into a tree. There had to be something that existed before the so-called "big bang," for, if there was nothing, what banged against what? There has to be something inside the life each of us lives—some Power that we call God. Without that Power, these bodies would quickly decompose. And since that Power is Omnipresent, it must be our consciousness that changes. It must be that when our focus is self-centered we only see ourselves and cannot perceive the Oneness of life as it emanates from that One Source. When the "I" holds on, keeps control of consciousness, we block out the potential Consciousness of God.

We could no more be separate from the Source of life than a ray of sunlight could exist separate from the sun. So how did we forget? How did we isolate ourselves? What is this "I" that distracts us, blocks us, blinds us, numbs us, torporizes us and keeps us from the Truth? What keeps us from knowing that Truth which would cure our loneliness, soothe our anger, relieve our anxiety and remove all frustration?

Here is an explanation, a parable Bawa tells, that illustrates how it is we have forgotten who we really are:

Suppose you planted a seed from a tree and watched it grow until it was tall enough to accept a graft. Then, suppose you grafted a branch from some other kind of tree onto that first tree. Suppose you pruned away any other branches but the new branch you had grafted on.

Since you pruned away all the branches that grew from the original tree, eventually, as the branch you grafted on grew and sprouted more branches, the tree would take on a new identity. All its branches, all its leaves, all its blossoms and all its fruit would all be from the branch you had grafted on. So the mature tree would look like the tree you had taken that branch from. It would not look like the tree the seed had come from. Its fruit would not have the taste that was the potential within that original seed.

That is what has happened to us. There was an Original Seed from which we were born. Had it not been tampered with, our lives might have produced different fruit. We might have a different consciousness. There might be a different knowing. But this "I" was grafted on by the constant concentration on "yours" and "mine" all around us. "Your brother eats his peas, why don't you?" "I got a 100 on my test, what did you get?"

Your race, my race, your religion, my religion, your kind, my kind, all have been grafted on. That arrogance, that fear, that pride, that depression, all result from what has been grafted on. That is not the Power that was in that seed. That is not our roots.

Just as the tree knows its own roots no matter what leaves and fruit are growing on the outside, we know our roots. We know what was in that seed. We know that Power is within every seed. That Power is within every energy. That Power is within everything that has life and everything that nourishes life. It may be hidden from our consciousness, but we know that Power. That Power is our True Roots. That is who we really are.

If we can prune away everything that has been grafted on and everything that grew from what was grafted on, we can become that Original Intention. We can blossom and bear the intended fruit.

That Power out of whom all creation comes—that Formless Power we call God—planted a seed that was to become a Human Being "created in His own image." The qualities of mankind were meant to resemble the Qualities of God. Those Qualities are the intended fruit.

Look at the Quality of Divine Justice. Look at the way in which the Creator has provided the appropriate food for each form of life. God does not ask the fish in the sea to live on the fruit of the land. That Divine Justice is God's Grace. Yet, God also has provided man with the potential Wisdom to enable him to also bear such Justice—to provide each according to his needs. When sand gets in your eye, your eye automatically waters and washes the sand away. That is Divine Justice. It is not possible for a particle of sand to bribe the tear ducts so that it can remain as an irritant. Man, too, has the potential Wisdom to administer such Justice.

Look at the Quality of Divine Compassion. When it rains, the rain nourishes the weeds as well as the flowers. That is Divine Compassion. That is God's Grace. When you cut your hand, calcium rushes from everywhere in your body to help heal the wound. The calcium in your foot doesn't decide that since the cut is in the hand it won't bother to go. That is Divine Compassion. That is God's Grace in action. Mankind, too, should be capable of such Compassion.

Did we grow according to the potential within that Original Seed? Did we grow bearing the Qualities of Love, Compassion, Justice, Truthfulness, Patience, Forbearance, and the understanding that each life is as important as our own? Or did we have gardeners in our lives who pruned away God's Qualities and grafted on the qualities of greed, envy, selfishness, blind ambition, lust, deceit, anger, frustration and arrogance? We have learned to seek status, position and power in the world instead of Unity with our fellow beings. We have learned to measure success in material possessions instead of in Contentment.

As a result of this type of grafting, we even describe ourselves according to what we think we have become instead of what we really are in our secret roots. This grim self-assessment is bound to cause inner conflict and frustration. No matter how successfully we have born fruit from those branches that have been grafted on, we know—we sense from somewhere deep within our being—that we are not "ourselves."

Yet, we so strongly identify with what we have become that, when someone asks us about ourselves, we usually begin answering by telling what we do. We say, "I am a student," or, "I am a writer," or, "I am a teacher." Then we might say that we are married or single, that we have children, what kind of house we live in, what hobbies we enjoy, even what political philosophy we espouse. In short, we describe all the things about us that are subject to change. We describe the "I" of us; that which we have learned from the branch-grafting farmers of the world—our parents, teacher, preachers and friends.

We do not describe that changeless thing which also is there. Yet, how many times in a lifetime do we find ourselves saying, "I just want to be myself!" How many times do we complain, "I can't be myself with those people!"

If we are ever to become Content, we first must discover who we are. We must discover what that Unchanging Essence is within us. And if we discover that, we also will have discovered that Power which we call God, because only God is Unchangeable.

Everything in the world changes. Today there are mountains where once was water and there are oceans where once were mountains. Yet, that Power out of which all creation has come is Unchanging. Anything that has a beginning will change, and eventually will die. Change itself is the death of whatever existed before the change. But that Power out of which all creation came is an ongoing endless Power. That does not change. And since God is the only thing that doesn't change, anything that doesn't change must be some aspect of God—some aspect of that Power.

When you say, "I want to be myself," aren't you referring to some aspect of yourself that does not change? Isn't there something that you feel deep within your very roots that has always been there even though your body, mind and emotions have gone through countless changes?

That Essence of you that does not change is of the Essence of God. It is that Unchanging Essence that truly can be called a Human Being. It is that Unchanging Essence that is created in "His own image." And He—that Power—is its rightful owner. It is a ray of His Light. It is our very Soul.

It is that Soul that is buried. It is the potential hidden within the Soul that would have become the intended fruit. It is from the Soul that the Divine Qualities were meant to emerge.

Until we realize our Soul, it lies hidden like a diamond in the rough. And, in a certain respect, the Soul is to God as the diamond is to sunlight. We usually take sunlight for granted. Only rarely do we notice the glory of light itself. Yet, if we hold an absolutely pure, perfectly faceted and proportioned diamond up to the light, it bursts with luminous radiation and seems on fire with spectral colors. Our eyes can only sense the dazzling beauty of light as it pours out from the prism of the diamond.

God and the Soul are like that. We appreciate God's Power. There would be no life without it. Yet we cannot say that we can see the beauty of God's Grace except as we see it radiate through the Soul of a Pure Human Being. The prophet, the saint, the illumined being, all display the glory of God's Grace. They awe us with the magnificence and beauty of Divine Compassion, Divine Love, Divine Justice. Through them we sense the incredible brilliance of His Light.

Each human being is born with that potential within his Soul. That is what we must look for. That is our task; our cardinal duty.

A diamond does not show the beauty of light while it is buried in the ground. Nor does it show that true potential beauty in its rough form. First we must cut away any extraneous materials that have adhered. Then we must cut out any imperfections it may contain. Then we must facet it into the ideal shape required to reflect 100% of the light. Even then, we still have to clean it periodically.

Thus it is with the Soul of human beings. This body is the earth, and before we can even begin the process of reflecting God's beauty, we must cut away all attachment to this body and its appetites. Then we must search for and burn out the flaws that may be deep-seated within our hearts. As some diamonds are flawed by carbon deposits deep in their interior, we may have developed the characteristics of greed, anger or deviousness. We may have dark areas in our lives. We may have qualities that embarrass us; traits that cause us guilt.

Yet, even if we succeed in cutting away such flaws, the work is not finished. Just as the diamond must be faceted, we must shape our *lives* in such a way as to most ideally reflect God's Grace. It is not enough to cut out the impurities. We must put into action those Qualities that will ideally shape our lives. We must become Compassionate; we must have Patience; we must live Truthfully; we must Love each being as we love our own lives.

These are the actions that will transform us so that we can reflect God's Light. Having been transformed, our constant attention to God and our constant Trust in God keeps the transformed life—that Soul—perfectly polished.

This self-discovery, this cutting away of our impurities and this shaping and polishing is our responsibility. Everything else is God's Duty. When we have done our duty, then God's Grace and God's Intention burst forth from our lives as automatically as light radiates from the perfectly proportioned diamond.

Of course, this transformation is easier to talk about than to accomplish. It cannot be done simply by reciting prayers or mantras, nor simply through a meditation technique, nor through strict adherence to a diet, nor through psychoanalysis or any other therapeutic technique.

We all know "religious" people who are selfish or quick to anger. We all know men and women who have gone through countless drug trips, psychoanalytic experiences, primal screams, nude marathons, guru courses, mantras, meditation techniques, EST week-ends and tantric exercises, and still they cannot be said to reflect God's Grace.

It is one thing to read that the relationship of a Human Being and God can be of such perfect harmony as that between a diamond and the light. It is another to find that inner diamond, free it from its surrounding impurities, shape it, facet, and surrender it to God.

Yet, such is God's Intention. And God has provided us with the Wisdom needed to fulfill that Intention.

It may be necessary for those rare teachers such as Bawa Muhaiyaddeen to come as reminders of that Intention. But we are responsive because that memory is interwoven within our very Essence. If we follow that remembrance closely and with unwavering Determination, we can rediscover who we are. And when we discover who we are, we realize that we are not separate from God's Intention. And when we rediscover God's Intention, then we rediscover God. And then there is only One.

III
What Are Our Obstacles?

If it is God's Intention that we live in Perfect Harmony with His Radiant Power, why is that capacity to reflect His Light so hidden?

Consider this explanation: In order to grow rice you need water. Yet, contained within the water will be the spore for weeds. So there is no way to grow rice without weeds also growing. If no farmer tends the rice field, the weeds can become a formidable obstacle. They grow quickly and easily, generate their own seeds, these seeds take root, and soon, the weeds choke out the rice.

So the farmer who wants to grow rice knows that he must pull out whatever weeds sprout before they germinate and take over the field.

It is that way in our own lives. This body is the farm. God's Qualities can blossom on this farm. But contained within the elements of the body will be the spore for weeds that if left unattended, can become formidable obstacles. These weeds can choke out any possibility of God's Grace maturing within this life. So we must develop the discrimination needed to recognize weeds and we must have the Determination to pull those weeds as they sprout so that they have no opportunity to spread and take over this field.

If, as often is the case, your field has become overrun with weeds, it will require a great deal of work to prepare an open space in which God's Truth can grow. But once that task is completed, the work becomes much easier. You need merely stay alert and pull the tiny new weeds as they appear.

So let us examine the variety of weeds that are likely to take root in our lives. Only if we fully understand their source can we be sure to recognize them as weeds regardless of the limitless variety of ways in which they may appear.

There are three categories of such obstacles, or weeds. There is the obstacle of karma (inherited tendencies), the obstacle of maya (all illusions) and the obstacle of arrogance (the attachment to the "I").

Look at karma first. Don't confuse the karma of this birth with impressions you may have of previous births. The idea of reincarnation may be the greatest excuse that has ever been invented for not doing what you must do now. It is essential for you to decide whether or not you are willing to do over again all that you have had to go through up to now. If you are willing to repeat every painful experience of childhood and adolescence, then go ahead and embrace the idea of rebirth. Pretend that it doesn't matter whether you do it this time around. But if you suspect that there is no guarantee that you will be any stronger in character the next time than you are now, perhaps you should take a different approach.

Think of it this way: People already tend to blame their present weaknesses on things that happened to them in childhood. Now if you carry all those weaknesses with you into the next birth, and then add a few more during that childhood, and carry that accumulation on, wouldn't your chances of achieving a state of Purity get weaker instead of stronger?

It is better for you to concern yourself with your present karma and learn how to transcend that—and forget about past or future lives.

You are born with karma even if you were never born before. You inherit it through the bloodline. Certain of the character traits of the father and mother, and their fathers and mothers, and their fathers and mothers, are passed on from generation to generation.

Besides the genetic patterns passed on to succeeding generations, the specific emotional state of the parents at the time of conception affects the semen and ova from which the fetus is formed. Emotions such as arrogance, fear, passionate lust, anxiety, revulsion and the like cause a biological change measurably recorded in the bloodstream. The semen and ova are formed from the blood and carry this record into the new child.

So, whether you think of it as karma, racial memory, the collective subconscious, heredity or a carry-over of the emotional state of the parents at the time of conception, no one born of germ plasm is free from the chore of having to transcend built-in characteristics before he can reach that state in which the Original Seed that God planted—that Soul that can reflect God's Grace—can blossom.

Bawa often says, "Only animals have karma. Human Beings have no karma."

But by "Human Being" Bawa means that person who has conscious obedience to the Unchanging and Unchangeable Essence of life. When we cut our attachment to our own bodies and the emotions, desires, fears, angers and frustrations that grow out of that body, we also sever karma. Karma cannot exist in the Soul. It cannot grow in that Formless

Place. Just as weeds need earth in which to take root, inherited characteristics need the flesh and blood of the body. The Soul always remains Pure. More importantly, the Soul always contains within it the Wisdom through which we can transcend the body.

Remember, no one is born without karma and no one is born without the remedy for karma. The all-knowing Creator gave us eyelids that automatically blink to ward off damage to the eyes. He gave us bone marrow that automatically produces antibodies to ward off disease. We automatically cough to expel mucous. We automatically retch to expel spoiled food. Would that same Creator rob us of that inner Wisdom needed to evaluate our karma, see the mistakes it causes, learn from those mistakes, and move on?

There are, within each human being those levels of Wisdom necessary to see the dangers caused by inherited characteristics, or karma, and to avoid those dangers as easily as we react when a horn blows in traffic. That Wisdom is built into the Soul itself, just as our nervous system is built into the body. It speaks to us with a soundless inner voice. If we could hear our own inner voice and obey it, karma would have no influence on us whatsoever.

We already may know about that inner voice. We may have heard it clearly at one time or another in our lives. But, more often, we drown it out with activity. From the time we get up in the morning until we go to bed at night we fill our lives with noise. Radio, television, stereo, idle chatter, games and preoccupation with ambition, all rob us of the opportunity to hear ourselves.

Most of us are so afraid of quiet, we will do anything to avoid it. We will read the back of a cereal box while eating breakfast alone if there is nothing more interesting available to distract us. We will occupy our rare idle time in sometimes obviously ridiculous ways rather than be alone with that inner voice. At night, we may even get out of bed and get something to eat or find something to read in order to avoid listening to that inner voice. Why?

Because that inner voice, that Vibration of Wisdom that comes from the Soul, can speak only the Truth. It comes from an Unchanging and Unchangeable Source, so only Truth can emanate from it. When we become conscious of its Vibration, we simultaneously become conscious of how something false in our lives compares with that Truth. If we are making mistakes in our lives, if we are heading in directions that can cause us danger or harm, that comparison becomes a warning. It is our conscience. It is an insistent alarm system.

Yet, we may be so arrogant in our defiance of any and all authority, that we don't even want to be lectured by our own Soul!

Oh, after some unpleasant consequence we might even admit, "I knew that would happen. I knew it." And we probably did, but we weren't paying attention. Or, if we were, we ignored the warning from our inner voice. We just didn't want to hear about it.

That's arrogance.

There is no need to feel guilty or embarrassed by our past arrogance. We are all born with that tendency. It is part and parcel of the self-preservation instinct. We simply need to harness it. We simply must learn that most self-preservation reactions are automatic and without intelligence. Think of self-preservation instincts as a horse. It can be quite pleasant to ride a horse on a trail through the woods. But a horse running wild through a department store would be quite another matter. Like that, self-preservation instincts become arrogance when they emerge in inappropriate places.

For example, an infant must bite its mother to get its milk. That is self-preservation. Once the child gets its teeth and can eat solid food, if he insists on biting his mother's breast, that is arrogance.

In how many ways are we still biting long after we have gotten our teeth? To fully understand our symbolic biting, first look at our built-in reactions to real danger.

During any stress or fear situation, the autonomic nervous system is activated, adrenalin shoots into the body generating abnormal amounts of energy, sensitivity to pain decreases, and we become prepared to take on the danger or flee it. Fight or flight are the two primal responses.

When man lived in the jungles and he had to deal with natural predators for his very survival, these self-preservation instincts were essential. There still may be times when they are necessary. But for the most part, we no longer face the physical dangers our forebears feared hundreds of thousands of years ago.

Yet, we still may react to a threat to our ego the way a caveman might have reacted to a saber-toothed tiger!

If someone hurts our feelings, we respond by wanting to run away or do battle. If we decide that we need a certain amount of respect in order to feel secure, any threat to our status is treated as though it were a threat to our lives. Jealousy and envy also are inappropriate self-preservation reactions, or arrogance. The frustration we feel when we cannot get something we want is also arrogance.

If we want a certain job, or a car, a piece of chocolate cake, or quiet while we are watching television, we react to any threat to what we want with fear or anger—the primeval signals for fight or flight.

Why are we likely to be tricked into reacting with arrogance to things which really are no threat to our self-preservation? Why do we so confuse the things we desire or the status we desire with actual survival that we arrogantly ignore even our own inner voice?

Our confusion is caused by the torpor that results from what Bawa calls "maya"—the illusion of duality. For as long as our attention is riveted on the illusion of our having a separate individuality, we will also be enamored by everything and anything that can support or gratify the imaginary individuality—thus perpetuating and strengthening the illusion.

Just as the Wisdom exists within the Soul to warn us of mistakes we might make as a result of karma, that same Wisdom can enable us to harness our self-preservation instincts and prevent them from transforming into arrogance. That same Wisdom can point out to us the Unity of Life that is God's Effulgence. When we identify with that inner voice, we see clearly that we are not separate any more than the ray of light is separate from the sun.

It may be that as very tiny infants, during the first few months of our lives, we understand that these bodies are only the houses in which we live. But as our sense awareness develops we became distracted.

Just as a magician (illusionist) distracts his audience with his left hand while he performs his trick with his right, our five senses—needed to preserve the body/house—show us only the left hand of reality. So the moment we are able to focus our eyes as infants, we become fascinated by glitters.

Inadvertently, our parents help reinforce the illusion. The baby cries to be let out of the playpen, but Mother has work to do. So she gives the baby a toy that glitters or makes an amusing sound. The child becomes spellbound by the toy and forgets why he was crying.

As we get older, we take over the parent's role and find our own toys to keep ourselves spellbound and distracted from pursuing a real solution to our discontent. And in this technological age, there seems no limit to the varieties of toys we can create. Recently, the Internal Revenue Service ruled that private jet planes cannot be considered a business expense unless used for flights long enough to justify the additional cost of such fast planes. The theory of one IRS official is: "Private jets are rich men's toys."

We didn't have to invent so many toys to distract ourselves. Everything we see, hear, taste, touch and smell is an illusion. Nothing that changes is true. That which is true has always been true and always will be. The Truth is not something that appears to be true today but will change by tomorrow and, therefore, will be true no longer.

Until we see that essential Truth that unifies all of creation, until we know and identify with life itself, we will be subject to the torpor of maya.

We cannot see that Truth with our eyes or hear it with our ears. We cannot touch something that is a Formless, Limitless, All-Pervasive, Omnipresence. Our senses can show us only the world of form—the world of change.

If we wish to see Unchanging Truth, we must see it with an instrument that also is of that same Essence—that same Unchanging Nature.

We can use instruments made of the elements to see those things that have been created out of the elements. But if we wish to see that All-Pervasive Truth that is the Essence out of which all creation comes, then we first must discover that instrument within us that is capable of seeing it.

When we discover that, then it will enlighten us as the sun lights up the sky. Bawa calls that Truth which can see the Truth, "Divine Luminous Wisdom." And that is what we must seek.

But first we must realize that it is not hidden from us. We are hiding from it.

IV
WHAT IS WISDOM?

SUPPOSE THE EARTH stopped rotating. Suppose you grew up only having seen the night sky. You, no doubt, would become quite attached to the stars and the moon.

Now, suppose someone described to you something you had never seen called the sun. Suppose he tried to explain the brilliance of the sun and the clarity that would result from the light it brought; the wonders of everything you would see; and how different everything might seem. Suppose he told you that all you had to do to realize that sun and its light was to cut, completely, your attachment to the stars and the moon. Suppose, to help you cut that attachment, he also told you that once the sun came, the stars and moon would fade away.

Chances are, such talk would frighten many people, seem utterly foolish to others, and inspire only a few. And of those who were intrigued enough to at least want to see the sun, fewer still would be able, Determinedly, to cut their attachments to the stars and the moon. "After all," people might protest, "they shine so beautifully in the night sky and we use the stars to chart our way when we travel and to foretell the future and for so many things. How can we cut that kind of attachment?"

Yet that is very much the type of thing we are being asked to do. Just as the stars shine only in darkness, the countless billions of glitters of maya in the world also shine only in the darkness of our own ignorance of the Truth. If that Divine Luminous Wisdom were to come, it would dispel the darkness of ignorance just as the sun dispels the darkness of night. And the hypnotic power of all that now enthralls us would fade. The attractions would lose their mesmerizing glitter. Moreover, just as the sun always shines and it is the earth that rotates away from the sun to cause its own period of darkness, the effulgent Grace of God's Truth—that Divine Luminous Wisdom—is also constantly radiating, although we rotate our consciousness away from it.

This is not a physical turning. God's Truth is not in a place. It is not something that can be located inside of us nor outside us. It is an All-Pervasive Essence. And when our consciousness is focused elsewhere, it is our consciousness that has rotated away from the Truth.

The human being has seven levels of consciousness: Perception, awareness, intellect, judgment, subtle wisdom, Divine Analytic Wisdom and Divine Luminous Wisdom.

Perception is experienced even by the newborn infant. The child experiences touch, taste, sound and smell; and within a few days, it begins to see. Even rocks and minerals have a kind of perception. Scientific tests have shown that minerals and metals experience stress and react to it. They feel.

The infant, however, soon develops awareness. That is, he can distinguish between warm and cold, a pleasing sound and a disturbing one, a sweet taste and a sour taste. If you pinch the child's foot, he will know that it is his foot that was pinched and not his hand. He will begin to recognize the scent and sound of his mother and to distinguish his mother from a stranger. Similarly, even plants have this second level of consciousness. Experiments have been conducted in which plants were wired to polygraph equipment (lie-detector machines). Then a student was told to kill one of the plants by beating it with a baseball bat. Later, a dozen students were asked to enter the room one by one. The needles on the polygraph equipment did not move until that student who had beaten one of the plants to death came in. Then all the needles began to oscillate violently. Plants have awareness.

The human being, however, also has intellect. We are able to store the information we collect from each and every experience into the computer bank we call the brain. Then, as in a computer, if we ask a question such as, "What is the way home?" the memory of a previous trip—each turn we took and each thing we saw along the way—can be recalled. While the human being's computer bank is somewhat larger than the brains of most other animals, all animals have intellect. All animals can learn to go through a maze to get their food, for example.

But animals are limited to these first three levels of consciousness. Human beings have four more levels. Yet, because of the obstacles of karma, arrogance and maya, most of us stop growing at intellect.

We become totally and utterly dependent upon intellect and we even try to use intellect to discover the Truth contained within Divine Luminous Wisdom. This is like trying to understand intellect using only the level of consciousness we are calling perception. Perception can't see or hear intellect and intellect can't conceive of Divine Luminous Wisdom.

So before we even try to understand the next four levels of consciousness, we must understand how intellect and the mind work together to keep us in a state of torpor.

The mind is not the same thing as the intellect. The intellect is merely the computer. It has no volition of its own. It is merely an organ of the body, like the stomach or the lungs. It stores the information we feed into it, and it retrieves that information on demand. The programmer of the computer, the aspect of the human being that selects what will go into the computer and what should be requested from the computer, is the mind.

The mind is the servant of all the desires that grow out of the five senses. We have heard the expression, "People see what they want to see; people hear what they want to hear." We may recall a time when we also were tricked by our mind into seeing something that wasn't there, or not seeing something that was there.

The mind obeys desire, and the intellect receives only that information the mind lets through. And desire, unless controlled by Wisdom, has no more discrimination in a human being than in a dog. We, too, may sniff at and examine everything to see if it is something we want.

As a child, if we had one toy and saw another toy, we desired the second toy as well. As adults, if we have one car and see another car that looks desirable, we look longingly at the second car. We may have one mate and still ogle others. We may have status and position and still, envy the status and position of another. Such is the doglike nature of desire. And since desire rules over the mind, the mind remains in constant motion.

The mind cannot possibly obtain everything desire asks for. So the mind eventually learns to satisfy desire at least temporarily by projecting a kind of movie of the desired object. We see what the mind wants us to see.

Even when we go to a theatre to see a movie we know is make believe, we still cry at the sad parts, laugh at the funny parts and become frightened by the scary parts. We respond as though it were real.

So it is not surprising that we respond to the movies created by the mind and projected onto the screen of the world in which we live. The mind can splice together any scrap of film ever recorded and stored in the brain. If we want to feel powerful and intimidating, it will show us a film of frightened faces. If we want to feel exciting and attractive, the mind will project a film of adoration onto the faces of those around us. We see what we want to see.

If we want to look a certain way, the mind will even project its film on our own appearance. We talk the way we do because the mind selected the tone, the inflection, the vibration and everything else about our speech patterns. Of course, there may be physiological limits within which the mind must work, but it puts its film together from whatever is available. So the way we walk, gesture, dress, respond, laugh, cry, sing and dance are all a part of this film the mind creates.

Ironically, the mind gets its pictures of how to look, laugh, talk and so on from what it sees others doing. But the others also are acting out their homemade movies. So in a very real sense, we are projecting movies that we have filmed of other movies.

Stranger yet, even though we directed the filming, and we wrote the script, and we project ourselves as the star in this movie that we decided to create, we still can't satisfy desire and we complain about it.

A poet once said that out of despair comes enlightenment. Unfortunately, that isn't always true. All too often, despair only generates the need to create more complex movies, which, in turn, eventually lead to even more despair.

For example, despair often leads to a dogmatic belief in some economic doctrine, political system or to the rituals of religion. A person discovers that following every whim of desire has brought only misery, so he grabs some authoritative doctrine the way a drowning man might grab at a floating board. A new film of lofty values is projected onto the doctrine. The appearance of the reality of that film is reinforced by similar projections by others. Soon, such a person may become a fanatic.

We must understand that politics, economics, religions and philosophies have the same limitations as intellect. As long as we are still ruled by karma, arrogance, maya, mind and desire, what kind of political system can we create? What kind of religion? If we say there is only One God but we have no experience of God, we might just as well have said there is only one thingamajig. What's a thingamajig? What is God?

We can say that Jesus is the son of God, but again, we must understand what God is and how it is that God, who is Formless, could have a son. We must understand who Jesus is. Otherwise we are only parrots. We are only repeating what we have been told.

Religious doctrines or philosophical concepts are fed into the intellect and the mind takes these bits and pieces of information and splices them together with liberal doses of imagination based on countless other experiences and it creates a movie of God and Truth. It may create such a realistic film that we firmly believe it.

But belief, or faith, and knowing are not the same. I may so intensely want something to be that I believe it is so. I may insistently declare my faith in its being so. That faith may even cause me to overlook contrary evidence. For years I might see nothing that shakes my faith. But if that contrary evidence—that Reality—eventually breaks through my movie version of faith, my faith will shatter.

A crazy person can have absolute faith that his body is invincible. But his faith will be badly shaken the first time he gets hit by a car.

When we know something, it is because we have experienced the Truth of it. We know its Unchanging Essence. Then no doubts can occur. It no longer is necessary to cling to something we merely "believe in" with fanatical zeal. We don't have to keep inventing more and more movies to support the appearance of reality in the movies we already have filmed.

The person who has experienced God can withstand the ordeals of Job, and his Faith will not be shaken. Such a person would never feel that God had forsaken him, or that God was punishing him, or that God was angry at him. He would never experience despair.

God's prophets knew the Truth. They did not despair. But the religions that men created from their impressions of the messages of the prophets were not the same.

Each prophet brings a Truth as Pure as the spring water that spurts forth at the top of a mountain. But as that spring water travels down the mountain and forms a stream, it picks up certain amounts of silt and filth along the way. Then the animals come to drink from that stream and bathe in it and soil it. By the time the stream becomes a river, whole cities dump their waste and industrial poisons in it. Still, if we know what pure water is, we can extract the water by filtering away the impurities.

Thus it is with religions. Through the years each prophet's original message has become a movement and then a religion, and many impure thoughts and ideas have polluted it. Too many men have tried to make a living from religion and have added their narrow concepts to that original message. If we already know the Truth of that original message, we can extract it from any religion simply by filtering out the pollutants. But it is not a matter of "belief." We have to know.

That is why we must go beyond intellect. That is why all that enamors us in this movie world is called illusion. The glitter exists only in the darkness of our own ignorance—and ignorance exists only because we have not gone beyond the first three levels of consciousness. That also is why it is so urgent that we turn away from the night sky that keeps us mesmerized and turn toward that Divine Luminous Wisdom that will dispel that darkness. We must do it.

And we begin by employing judgment—the capacity to evaluate the condition of our lives. We must determine, for example, whether or not all our successes have brought us Contentment, or whether they resulted in even more tension and stress in our lives. We must evaluate our present state of well-being and see whether the various methods we may have employed to find peace of mind have actually produced Serenity. We must examine, honestly, those compulsive whims and desires that still cause us guilt or embarrassment and judge whether or not all our therapy, meditation, self-discipline or self-help techniques have actually enabled us to be happier with ourselves.

If we use our own good judgment, we might recognize that we are not yet seeing the Truth. We might see that we have been trapped into believing a movie which only seems real in the darkness.

Our own good judgment might show us that we are still blocked by the obstacles of karma, arrogance and maya. And as a result of this evaluation, we might realize that this fourth level of consciousness must be utilized constantly as a wise observer—a witness that will warn us if we are being tricked by movies.

A flower cannot be tricked into turning away from the sun. A tree in the shade of another tree will grow sideways for a time until it can reach its own share of the light; then it will grow upward. Yet, people will ignore their own good judgment—they will ignore that inner voice—and depend instead on the things they have learned in this movie world to find the Light within Divine Luminous Wisdom.

If that Power of Creation gave even a seedling tree the inner Wisdom necessary for it to find its sun, wouldn't God also have given us an inner voice to warn us with feelings of discontent when we are turning away from His Light? Wouldn't that same inner Wisdom provide us with feelings of Contentment and Peacefulness when we have turned toward that Light?

So if we employ our good judgment as a constant witness, we will begin to see the mistakes caused by our inherited tendencies; we will see the harm caused by arrogance; we will see how desire is a result of our illusions; we will see how our mind serves our desires; and we will see through our movies one by one.

Often this is a painful period. We don't always like what we see. But we must recognize that our self-pity is just another ploy of arrogance. Arrogance says, "This is who I am. Don't find fault with me. I can't help it. I have always been this way. Please don't criticize me."

If that doesn't work, arrogance will say, "You are crazy. This whole thing that you are doing is crazy. You are just stupid believing all this stuff about judgment and wisdom. I'm O.K., you're O.K. Stop judging me. Stop evaluating me. I'm fine just the way I am. I'm having fun. Don't you want me to have fun? Leave me alone."

If judgment persists in examining everything and pointing out the suffering as well as the fun, the discontent as well as the success, the lack of peacefulness as well as the exhilaration, the anger and frustration as well as the temporary satisfactions—if judgment continues to keep arrogance honest, then arrogance will begin to weep.

"Oh pity me," it will wail. "I try so hard to be good. I try so hard to seek God. I'm just no good. I'm rotten. Oh, I'm so miserable. But what can I do? I just keep doing the same things over and over again. Please, there is nothing I can do about it. Please pity me. Please give me something to make me feel better."

And in such ways, arrogance tries to seduce judgment into suspending itself. It tries anything it can—even the bitterest tears and self-flagellation—to stay in control.

But if judgment persists, it eventually sees that, indeed, arrogance cannot help itself. The mind cannot help itself. Desire cannot help itself. The elements will always glitter. The weeds of karma, arrogance and illusion will continue to grow for as long as this earth body lasts. All judgment can do is pull those weeds as it spots them. All good judgment can do is refuse to allow those weeds to mature and germinate so that even more weeds start growing. All judgment can do is keep a clear space in the soil of this life so that something else can grow.

The first sprout to grow in that open space will be a subtle wisdom. That subtle wisdom collects what judgment has seen and stores it within the heart, just as intellect stores those things collected by perception and awareness. There is a difference, of course, between the ways in which subtle wisdom and intellect function. Intellect stores everything that is brought to it—whether it is a lie or it is the Truth. It does not discriminate.

Subtle wisdom, however, examines what judgment has seen and discards anything that was born of karma, arrogance and illusion. It discards anything that changes. Subtle wisdom examines each thing that judgment sees, and it stores in the heart only those Essences within each thing that are Unchangeable. And in that way, subtle wisdom begins to fertilize the Original Seed.

Just as you must fertilize the soil and water it if you want that which grows from the earth to flourish, you must feed the Soul with the Qualities of God if you wish that which grows from the Soul to flourish.

The elements of the body can be categorized as belonging to five groups: Earth, water, fire, air and ether. So you must feed it with foods that are made of earth, water, fire, air and ether.

The Truth must be fed the Truth. God's Seed, which contains God's Grace and God's Power and God's Qualities, must be fed with God's Grace, God's Power and God's Qualities.

The essential Truth within each thing is God's Essence. That which doesn't change is God's Essence. That which changes is simply the form—the earth, water, fire, air, ethereal shell of it. Subtle wisdom extracts the Essence from each thing that judgment brings to it and stores that Formless Essence—that Grace—that Truth—in the inner heart.

And as a result of God's Grace, Divine Analytic Wisdom begins to grow.

Divine Analytic Wisdom is the representative of God. Subtle wisdom turns over everything of God's to Divine Analytic Wisdom and discards everything else. It severs all attachments to the "I" and surrenders to the Will of God.

Divine Analytic Wisdom explains the Will of God.

Just as a step-down transformer is needed in order for a house to utilize the electricity generated by a power plant, Divine Analytic Wisdom is needed before God's Power can emerge within a Human Being. This entire universe—including galaxies so distant that their light still has not reached the earth—is but a dot within the Power that we call God. Yet, the Essence of that Power, in its Completeness, exists within each and every creation of God.

Divine Analytic Wisdom explains that Essence. That sixth level of consciousness called Divine Analytic Wisdom, like the Essence of God, is not something that is unique to one individual or to one place in the world or to a particular time in history. It is as Timeless, Formless and Limitless as God. But it remains dormant, existing only as a potential, just as the tree is only a potential while it is still in the seed. When it grows within the heart of a Human Being, it acts as a transformer to bring us God's Vibration. It explains that Vibration so that it can be accepted.

This is how every prophet has been able to commune with God. God does not speak Hebrew or Latin. God does not speak English, Chinese, Hindi, Tamil or Sanskrit. God does not have a language, country or religion. God is an immeasurable Power. Each of the prophets heard the Vibration of that Power through the explanations of Divine Analytic Wisdom.

Divine Analytic Wisdom receives that Vibration from Divine Luminous Wisdom. Divine Luminous Wisdom is God's sun. That seventh level of consciousness is the Complete Effulgence of God. It is God's Light, the Power within that Light, the Grace within that Power, the Essence of Truth within that Grace, the Compassionate Qualities within that Truth, the Vibration within those Compassionate Qualities.

Divine Analytic Wisdom takes that Vibration and explains it to the Human Being of subtle wisdom who has "surrendered" his will to the Will of God.

And God wills to such a Human Being what he would will for Himself. That is why Bawa Muhaiyaddeen refers to such a Human Being as "Man-God, God-Man." That is why he says, "When 'I' am here, God is not; when God is here, 'I' am not."

It is natural that we should rediscover God by moving through these seven levels of consciousness step by step. To do so is simply to retrace the path through which we were created.

V

Where Do We Come From?

All discussions as to whether man evolved from monkeys, or fish, or from some form of plankton in the sea, are irrelevant. Such theories merely chart the supposed stages in the unfolding of the miracle called man. They cannot explain how or why such a miracle came to pass.

A pediatrician can tell us at what age a child should start to crawl, at what age his teeth will develop and at what age the child might start to talk. But the doctor cannot explain the miracle of growth from germ plasm to a mature human being.

So in this respect, the doctor knows no more about this miracle than the anthropologist. And they know no more than those scientists who speculate about the origin of the universe. Some embrace the "big bang" theory. Others consider the possibility of a pulsating universe, with alternating explosions and contractions. Yet, none can explain how the original explosion occurred.

In the time before creation, before there was anything, what banged?

If the mature tree is the hidden intention within the seed, is life the hidden intention within that original act of creation? More importantly, is the Realized Human Being the Creator's Intention?

Science must turn its back on such questions because they are outside its field. Science is confined to the measurable. If, in order to understand the intention of creation we seek to discover the cause of creation, we cannot look to science for answers since there was nothing to measure before creation.

In order to know who we are and where we came from, we ourselves must retrace our steps, so to speak, to that Indescribable Essence, or Pure Being, that is the Unmanifest, Formless Source of creation.

God has provided us with the map. Within this body, He has recorded the entire history of creation. And within the Essence of life, he has recorded the entire history of consciousness, all of the Wisdom of all of the prophets, His Complete Effulgence and all His Compassionate Qualities. And within the Effulgence of His Qualities, God resides.

So let us work our way back. First, examine the remarkable way in which this fabric that is the human form has been woven. In all of God's Limitless creation, there is nothing to compare with a Human Being.

Man contains within him the knowledge of the character of every animal that God has created. Other animals seem locked within the limitations of particular character traits. A lion always acts like a lion. He may be cunning and use precautions, but he never behaves like a frightened deer. Nor is a deer capable of the lion's ferocious behavior. Neither can be expected to act with the ponderous arrogance of an elephant; nor crawl into a shell like a self-protective turtle.

Yet a human being sometimes may act as aggressively as

a tiger, and sometimes like a scared rabbit, and sometimes like a bull in a china shop, and sometimes catatonically like a vegetable.

Now what gift has the Creator given the human being that allows him to know and experience the personalities of all of God's creations? And if God has given only to the human being this right to know all of His Creations, isn't it at least possible that God also would want the human being to know the Creator as well as His creations?

The human being not only can know all that is animate by looking within himself, he also can know all that is considered inanimate. Perceptible amounts of every one of the classic 92 elements that man has found in the earth's surface and in its rocks are also to be found within the human being.

During the human being's period of gestation, after the sperm cell and the ovum merge, he moves from a single cell to a fetus, to a form that resembles a tadpole, and on to a full formed human being. He retraces the entire history of life.

Man has within him the whole record of creation; all of it; everything that moves and everything that does not move; everything that is capable of sound and everything that is silent. Nothing has been left out.

Could it be, then, that God created such a remarkable creature without also instilling within it the Essence of that Original Power of Creation?

We have said that Essence is intermingled within life itself. Think about it. What is life? Life is not the material it wears as its house. Everything that lives wears a house built from five basic kinds of materials, or states of energy. And these five are natural enemies to each other.

All of God's creations, from viruses to birds, from fish to mammals, from grass to trees, are all made from the five basic materials of earth, water, fire, air and ether. That is, each house contains that which is solid, that which is liquid, that which is gaseous, some degree of temperature and the colors of ether.

The miracle of life can be seen in the fact that these diverse materials can coexist in any form. Where there is no life, liquids either will be absorbed by a solid or will dissolve the solid. Earth and water are natural enemies.

Where there is no life, water either will put out fire or will be boiled away and caused to evaporate by fire. Water and fire are natural enemies.

Where there is no life, fire can burn the earth and reduce it to ashes or be smothered by the earth. Fire and earth are natural enemies.

Where there is no life, fire can consume the energy in the air for its own sustenance or be blown out by too great a movement of air. Fire and air are natural enemies. Where there is no life, water evaporates into the air. Water and air are natural enemies to each other. Where there is no life, ether, the term physics uses for the transmitter of light and heat when integrated within the molecules of form, becomes instead the ethereal—the element within our upper atmosphere that gives it its blue color.

Where there is no life, earth merges with earth, water becomes just water again, fire is released to merge with the temperature of the planet, air rejoins the air, and ether returns to space.

Life is that which holds the elements together. Life is that Unchanging Essence that holds the elements in a cooperative partnership. Life is that sixth element which we sometimes call the Soul. Life itself is God's Grace. Life is what merges with the Power of God. The Soul is One with God. God's Grace knows God.

The seven levels of consciousness within the human

being enable us to know our history and to know His story. We can know the story of creation by looking within ourselves and we can know that Unchanging Essence by looking within ourselves. And when we know ourselves, we know God.

Scientists tend to bypass research into the Original and ongoing Cause of life by concentrating instead on the disciplines of chemistry, biology and physics—all of which measure what happens, not the Original Cause. Look, for example, at what science has discovered about all matter. What seems to us to be matter actually is energy moving within a pattern.

Light is a vibration. We can measure light waves. Even without measuring them, we can see. Sound is a vibration. We can measure sound waves. Even without measuring them, we can hear. Aromas also travel as waves of energy. Even without measuring them, we can smell. Similarly, without measuring the energy within matter, we take it for granted. We sit on a chair without concern about the energy of the molecules, and the atoms within the molecules, and the electrons, protons, neutrons and other subatomic particles within the atoms. But just as there are light waves and sound waves, every atom is an energy structure with a distinctive pattern of motion.

When we were youngsters, we would sit out on the front step and light slow-burning sticks we called "punks" to keep the mosquitoes away. It was great fun to whirl the lit end of the stick in a circle fast enough to make it look like a red ring in the air. In that same way, the energy of an atom, its electrons orbiting like a tiny solar system around the nucleus, gives us the impression of its being matter.

How do we explain energy? We can measure the motion of a particular energy, but motion itself is only a measuring device for time. We say that it takes a year for the earth to revolve around the sun, a day for the earth to rotate one full turn on its axis. Then we subdivide the day into hours, minutes, seconds and fractions thereof. In other words, we have used motion to create time. Without motion, there would be no way to measure time. Time itself, we are told, is a dimension.

What is a dimension? Scientists cannot measure the fourth dimension they speak of. And to say "all time is now" is as meaningless as to say "God is One" without ever having experienced that Oneness. In that respect, science has become like religion. Most of its devotees mouth the ritualistic words without genuine understanding of their meaning.

There must be a source from which any type of energy originates. We can create an explosion, but to do so we must use the materials that contain the explosive energies we need. We can produce electricity. But to power the electric generators, we need the energy that is contained within the fuel. We might use water power, coal, oil, a nuclear reactor or solar energy to generate the electricity. But there is a source from which all that energy comes.

Science is discovering that inside every atomic particle there are subatomic particles and sub-subatomic particles within those. Science is discovering that within every energy there is another energy and another energy within that. Science has not been able to discover an end to this type of research. Science has not been able to arrive at a conclusion—an Original Cause. Therefore, science cannot say there is no God.

Yet, that Original Power of Creation which we call God exists now as the Source of energy in every single atom as well as in every energy that is formless or nonatomic. God exists as the cause within every cell, and God exists as the cause within that which can be conscious of the cause.

The Human Being can be conscious of God even if he cannot measure God with the tools of science. If we can see light without measuring light waves; if we can hear sound without measuring sound waves; if we can sit on a chair without measuring the energy within its atomic particles, isn't it logical that we should be able to realize God's Power without trying to measure that Power? Isn't it logical that if God gave us the five sense with which to perceive His creation, that He also would have given us that sixth sense, that Divine Wisdom, with which to perceive His Essence? Aren't we experiencing life, the sixth element, the Soul, God's Grace, already?

We cannot experience life through a book, no matter how sacred some people consider that book. We cannot know what even a rose is like by reading a description of it. Similarly, we cannot pretend to know anything about God from having read about Him.

We must realize that even the Bible, the Koran, the Upanishads, the Vedantas and every other holy treatise that has ever been written are about as close to God as is the world of form. To know God through His creation, we must go within form to discover the energy of that form, and then within the energy to discover the Power that is the Source of that energy, and then within the Power to discover God. Similarly, to know God through inspired books, we must go within the holy book to discover the actual words that came from the prophets who inspired the writing of the books. Then we must go within the prophets' words to discover that sound the prophets heard within their hearts; then within the sound to discover its meaning; then within the meaning to discover the Vibration from which that meaning was taken; then within the Vibration to discover that Power that was the

Source of that Vibration; and then within that Power to discover God.

We have been saying that when we know ourselves we know God; that God's Story is interwoven within the life itself. We are His book. We are the form of His story. No story, no science, no book, no explanation can have real meaning for us unless we see it and understand it as part of our direct experience of our life.

Like others who have come before him, Bawa Muhaiyaddeen uses words to describe creation. The meaning of his words must be examined within our own hearts. Here, paraphrased, is Bawa's explanation:

In the time before time, in that timeless period before creation, God was alone in darkness. There was nothing other than that Unmanifest Power—neither form nor formless. Then God began to reflect upon Himself. This period of reflection in the timeless period before creation is immeasurable. The Power of His gaze inward upon Himself is immeasurable. It grew in intensity over this Limitless expanse of the beginningless beginning until the intensity of His examination erupted spontaneously as Light.

This Light spread as an Effulgence and then was reabsorbed into God. God reabsorbed His Effulgence to examine and discover its meaning. This Light which came from the intensity of God's examination of Himself was in turn reabsorbed so that it could be understood. Then, because of the intensity of this examination, Light emerged again. Several times this Effulgence appeared and was reabsorbed.

Then God saw that wherever this Light moved as it radiated outward from Him, it dispelled the darkness and that was good. So God asked the Effulgence, "Who are you? Before this, I was alone in the darkness. Now, wherever you have gone, you have dispelled the darkness. Who are you that now can be seen where there was nothing but darkness before?"

The Effulgence answered, "My Father, I have been born from You. I am the Light that has issued forth from You as a result of Your meditation upon Yourself. So I am You. Without You I am nothing." Thus, the Effulgence surrendered itself completely unto God.

Then God saw that wherever His Light intermingled with the world of darkness, shadows appeared. And as a result of the Power of His Effulgence, these shadows began to pulsate with life.

Then the Effulgence explained, "As I came from within You, the Light came from within me and the life came from the Essence of that Light. My Father, but for You, nothing would exist."

Then God instructed the Effulgence, "I shall form a being from this darkness that has been discarded and it shall be given life. And within the life I shall place the Essence of Light so that it can serve as an explanation of life. And within the Essence of Light I shall place the Essence of my Effulgence so that it can serve as an explanation of the Light. And within my Effulgence I shall reside as an explanation."

Thus was the True Human Being created. From the time of creation itself, before evolution or anything else that science has theorized about, even before the form of the first man emerged, there was that agreement. That is the covenant God has with man. From the time before Adam, it has been arranged that man should be able to know himself and, therefore, God, through that same self-examination through which God knows God.

Only after this agreement was reached did the creation of the world of form begin. Out of that Light, ether came to transmit the Light. And out of the energy of that transmission by ether, air came. And out of the rubbing together of those molecules of air, heat or fire came. And out of that interplay of air and temperature, water came. And out of the interplay of water and temperature, earth came. And out of the interplay of all these elements with the earth, living forms that would serve as food emerged. And only then, when food existed to nourish still unmanifest beings, did intelligent life emerge. Only then was the Human Being given form so that he could carry out that covenant. Except for this covenant with man, nothing else would have been created.

Man is God's representative. God has no form. God has no arms and legs, no shape or color that can be seen. God is realized through His Qualities as they emerge from the Realized Human Being. So God has given man His entire Treasury. All His Wealth, all His understanding, all His Qualities, God has placed in man. God is man's True Wealth. Man is God's Treasury.

You must see God within your heart. You must see the Truth of this explanation of creation within the Truth of your life. You must go inside this explanation and experience the Vibration from which it comes. If you try to analyze the words that were used with the intellect, your understanding will be limited to the level to which intellect can rise.

For example, someone who had just listened to Bawa's explanation of creation asked, "Bawa, all energies occur as a result of some kind of friction. Even energy that is inherent within an element requires some kind of friction in order to allow it to emerge. If God was alone in darkness when He gazed upon Himself, what was it that rubbed against what for that Effulgence to emerge?"

Bawa answered, "When Grace rubs against Perfection, the Power of God comes."

That Essence which is God's Grace already exists within

us as life. Now it is up to us to understand and become that Perfection. When they coexist, then God's Power can be realized.

VI
Is There Perfection?

IT COULD BE SAID THAT God is the Only Perfect One. As long as duality exists, as long as there is an "I" and a "You," there cannot be Perfection.

If we are to achieve that Perfection, then there is no choice but to surrender, totally, to that conscience that resides within the heart—that subtle wisdom that can distinguish between right and wrong. We must, little by little, discard what is wrong—that which emanates from karma, arrogance and illusion—and keep only what is right—that which is of the Essence of that Original Source.

When we surrender to that inner voice, that conscience that grew in the space provided for it by our good judgment, when we are obedient only to that subtle wisdom, then subtle wisdom can surrender to the Soul—that Divine Analytic Wisdom. As that process takes place, as subtle wisdom cuts attachments to everything that is changeable and gives devotion only to that Unchanging Essence, we begin to lose our sense of separateness. That illusion of duality begins to fade in the Light of Wisdom. Our entire being becomes obedient to that Divine Analytic Wisdom and, in that state, there is no duality.

We must understand that there is not more than One Divine Analytic Wisdom, just as there cannot be more than One Truth. If, like oil and water, two things that are called true cannot merge one within the other, then one must be false.

Light will always merge with light. If you turn on two lamps, at any spot where the light from the two lamps meet, they will merge. You will not be able to look at that spot and determine which portion of light came from which lamp. Light is light.

Similarly, Truth is Truth. There is not more than One. And that Quality of the Truth which makes it understandable to Human Beings also is unique. Wherever Divine Analytic Wisdom is in operation, it will be the same. There is not more than One, though it may appear in Realized Human Beings who are thousands of miles or even thousands of years apart.

Consider, for example, the growth rings in a tree. As they continue up the trunk of the tree to where the trunk separates into branches, they may seem to separate. That is, if we cut a cross section out of one branch and another cross section out of another branch, the two cross sections might give the appearance of having separate growth rings. Even the growth patterns visible in each cross section might appear different.

Yet within the context of the tree, they are not separate at all. If you hit the root of that tree with a shovel, the shock would be felt by every branch, every twig, every leaf. The growth rings are a continuous entity. All that is known and experienced by the growth rings in the trunk is also known and experienced by the growth rings in the tiniest twig. The energy derived from the sun permeates every branch—thick or thin. The nourishment taken from the earth by the roots is known by the growth rings in the trunk and in every branch.

As with the growth rings, the Divine Analytic Wisdom, man's Soul, that channel through which we commune with God, is not different in you than it is in me. And it receives that Complete Effulgence of God which we are calling Divine Luminous Wisdom. It is at One with that as surely as the growth rings anywhere in the tree are at one with the tree.

And Divine Luminous Wisdom is at One with God. You cannot cut away that which emanates directly from God, just as you cannot separate the sunlight from the sun. You cannot catch a ray of light in a box, close the lid and believe the ray of light is in the box. Only darkness will be in the box. You cannot separate light from its source. Similarly, you cannot close yourself off from that Divine Luminous Wisdom and expect its Light to remain within you. You cannot separate that consciousness from God.

The Light and the Source of the Light are One.

God and His Effulgence are One.

That Effulgence and its meaning are One.

When you surrender to that meaning within your own heart; when you obey that inner Guru that is Divine Analytic Wisdom; when you listen to that explanation and discard what must be discarded and keep what must be kept, then you are in a state of Perfection. You are One with God. You have merged with God as completely as the raindrop merges with the ocean.

There is no way you can hold onto your illusion of individuality and know God. Only God can know God. You must become the Quality of God that can know God's Qualities. You must reach that state of Perfection. You must go within your heart and obey only that conscience.

There is no other way.

Unless we retrace the steps we took to reach our separated condition and let go of each thing we have collected along the way, we will not be able to realize the total Contentment that exists within that Perfection. Instead, we will be trapped by those very attachments.

There is a story that illustrates just how foolish our attachments may be:

A boy who lived in the jungle wanted to capture a monkey and train it as a pet. So he took a handful of corn kernels and went looking for a tree with a knothole just small enough to suit his purpose. When he found such a tree, he deposited the corn kernels in the knothole and went home. The knothole he selected was just wide enough for the monkey to slip his hand in if he bunched his extended fingers together as tightly as possible. Once the monkey grabbed the corn kernels in his fist, however, he would not be able to extract his hand from the hole without letting go of the corn. His fist would be too wide.

Of course, the boy found the monkey with his hand still in the tree when he returned. The monkey simply couldn't let go of the corn once he had it in his grasp.

We may be as foolish in some respects as that monkey. Holding on to that very illusion of individuality that separates us from God, we go in search of God. We are like the fish that is looking for water.

As long as we seek the Truth without letting go of our attachments to things, to people, to ideas, to religions, to political groups, to philosophies, to status and position, to the arts and to sciences and to all the things we have created out of the elements, and to anything that can be perceived through the five senses, we will be trapped by the illusion of duality. And as long as we are trapped by illusion, our search for God will be equivalent to a fish looking for water.

When we cut the power of that illusion by giving up our attachments, we will not have to look for God. We will realize, finally, that God has always been as close to us as life itself.

There is no method or technique we can use to discover and merge with God that also allows us to remain in the illusion of separateness. "I" cannot look for God via any method.

The more we cherish some method that seems to give us pleasure or a degree of satisfaction, the more that method simply becomes another attachment.

Drugs certainly have to be looked at in this light. Most people are quite ready to dismiss drugs such as heroin, cocaine and amphetamines as not only ineffective as a vehicle for reaching God, but also as extremely dangerous. Even those who use such drugs are not prepared to defend their use on "religious" grounds.

Yet, the so-called psychedelic drugs—marijuana, hashish, peyote, mescaline, psylocibin, LSD and other hallucinogens—still attract users who genuinely believe that their drug-induced experiences are enlightening. Some users feel they have communicated with Jesus or with other prophets or saints while "high" on drugs. Some merely say that drugs have taken them through doorways to other, subtler realities. Some say they have actually experienced God while on a drug.

But really, all drugs can do is amplify your own movie. If the movie your mind usually projects can be compared with a black-and-white film shown on a small screen, the drug-induced movie might be a full color, 3D spectacular with wrap-around sound. But it is still a movie. It fills you with joy one moment, terrifies you the next, inspires tears of reverence one moment and raucous laughter the next, pulls you floatingly out of your body one moment and slams you heavily back the next.

God is not like that. In that communion with God there is no guilt, no paranoia, no sexual need, no hunger as there is during a drug experience. The glitters fade in the incredible brilliance of that communion with God. During a drug experience, everything that glitters, glitters more.

Consciousness must rise above the limitations of the senses in order to commune with God. Drugs actually prevent that from happening by exaggerating the appeal of sensuous things.

Fortunately, most people who take a drug eventually "come down." The drug wears off. Only a few are seriously damaged by a one-time experiment. But habitual drug users tend to live more and more in the fantasy world of their drug-induced movies and less and less in the level of reality that even intellect could show them. More importantly, the drug short-circuits the user's capacity to employ that fourth level of consciousness. His good judgment disappears.

Finally, drugs take a toll on the body as well. They are just one more pollutant to contend with in a world already overpolluted. It seems amazing that some of the same bright young people who first became aware of ecology and the need for a correct diet may still be so attached to their drug experiences that they continue to pollute their bodies in this way.

It only helps to demonstrate that adhering to a particular diet does not guarantee that you will become any closer to God. Hitler was a vegetarian.

It obviously is not enough simply to give up meat. We must stop living on the flesh of those we exploit. We must not kill another's spirit with our arrogance or with our jealousy. We must not try to dominate others and rob them of their life potential. We must not wound another person and hurt his heart with our anger.

If we could become True Vegetarians by avoiding even the subtle violence that damages another's potential, that would be progress. That would move us closer to the Compassionate Qualities of God. If we only avoid eating meat, that will only benefit the body.

Similarly, many people consider yoga exercises beneficial to the body. However, it also is true that many people have been treated by chiropractors, osteopaths, and surgeons as a result of physical injuries that were caused by practicing certain yoga postures. So if, for health reasons, you wish to practice yoga, take great care in selecting a teacher. Find someone who can fully understand the condition of your body.

If, for example, the vertebrae in your neck are not perfectly aligned, standing on your head could cause serious, perhaps permanent, damage. If certain yoga exercises are not practiced properly, nerves may be pinched, with severe pain and long-term damage. Even trained athletes, in ideal physical condition, sustain injuries to tendons, joints and nerves as a result of the accidental abuse of the body. So please take care before you exercise the body in an unusual way.

As for physical yoga exercises helping you to realize God, they are no more useful than pressing your eyeballs until you see stars, or sticking your thumbs in your ears until you can hear the gurglings of your own juices. The gurus who recommend such practices are not fools. They know the joy we get from playing with toys and they have given us our own bodies to play with as though they were the best toys of all. We pay them handsomely for the tricks they show us.

There are energies in each of the elements of your body that can be activated by certain practices. It is easy to become fascinated by the game of making these energies jump on command.

It is possible to learn how to make heat radiate out of your hands. It is possible to send your ethereal body to visit people in distant places. It is possible to make energy rise from your coccyx to the top of your head and enjoy the exhilaration that produces. It is possible, via certain meditation techniques, to hear voices or see what seem to be spiritual visions. Other techniques can be used to prolong the orgasm, and still others will block sensitivity to pain. You can learn to slow the heart beat and to hold your breath under water longer than any of your friends.

But none of these techniques can help you merge with God. None can give you lasting Peace and Contentment. The body contains so many energies you can play with. But these energies are only manifestations generated by this manifestation called the body. They are not that Essence. That Essence of life exists in all three worlds. This world of form, the world of God's Effulgence and within that Original Source. The energies of the body exist only in the world of form. We cannot realize God through something that does not exist except in this world of illusion. You cannot quench your thirst with the water from a mirage.

This also is why various psychotherapies are useless as a technique for understanding God. Like the use of drugs and like the psychic games we play with the body, the various types of therapy support and encourage people to concentrate on the "I."

Every therapist—with a degree or without—hopes to help his patient achieve peace of mind. There is no such thing as peace of mind. There is only Serenity and

Contentment in the Soul. The mind is not capable of being still Like the ocean, if the surface waves that the mind causes become calm, currents beneath the surface will pull you. And if these subconscious currents are released, there will be waves of activity on the surface again.

Unless we transcend karma, arrogance and illusion, we cannot find Peace. Our inherited characteristics still will predetermine certain responses. Our arrogance will keep us focused on the separations of "yours" and "mine," with all the envy, jealousy, anger and frustration inherent in such a view of life. And we still will be hypnotized by the countless glitters of illusion. Most therapists also believe in the illusions. They do not know that the Truth must exist in all three worlds. So while the therapist is helping us dump out those neuroses he can see, our minds form new neuroses. We never achieve Peacefulness.

We must cut our attachment to the body and its pains and pleasures. We must go beyond such a limited focus. That is why neither the extreme discipline enforced in some monasteries, ashrams and other organizations, nor the undisciplined, "let-it-all-hang-out" hippy life style help people understand God and reach Peace.

Neither life style, disciplined nor undisciplined, helps an individual cut his attachment to his own body. Both extremes heighten the amount of attention a person gives to his bodily functions.

It is one thing to fast, it is another not to be hungry. So the person who gives up eating in conformance with some discipline pays as much attention to the idea of food as does the glutton. The performance of any discipline forces us to pay attention to the discipline, not to God. The person who truly is obedient to his own inner voice is not performing a discipline.

It requires no discipline to pull your hand away from a hot stove.

The person we might call undisciplined is one who has simply so centered his attention on the world and its sensuous pleasures that he can no longer hear his inner voice. He can no longer feel the consequences of his mistakes because he is so distracted by the world and its glitters.

So performing rituals, methods, techniques and disciplines cannot get you to merge with God, and avoiding the performance of rituals, methods, techniques and disciplines cannot help.

To realize God, we must know what God knows. We must become that Truth in our thoughts and actions so that Truth will merge with Truth. We must become One with God by reshaping our lives so that our qualities and God's Qualities intermingle as completely as light merges with light.

VII
What Are God's Qualities?

If two violins are tuned exactly alike, and if you pluck a string on one, the vibration of the first violin causes a sympathetic vibration in the other. There will be no difference between the two, and the sound you will hear will be the result of both violins resonating as one.

In a similar way, when we are "in tune" with God, His Vibration and the Vibration of His instrument within our hearts become One Vibration. This is how that Power of Creation communicates with the Human Being, and this is how the Human Being communicates with God. No words are needed; no prayers or mantras need be recited; no ritual need be performed. When we are "in tune" with that Power that nourishes and enriches all life, our thoughts will be God's thoughts, our actions will be God's Actions, our love will be God's Love, our sense of justice will be God's Justice.

When our will is God's Will, the "I" will have vanished. Only God will exist.

The discord in our lives occurs when we are not "in tune" with that Primal Source of life. Indeed, the chaos in the world exists because we are all performing our own separate songs at once. Rarely do we even consult each other when selecting the principal "pitch" to which we tune our lives. Indeed, we are more like three-and-a-half-billion band leaders, each imploring others, "Get in tune with me!"

Some are more insistent than others. Political activists, missionaries, neighborhood bullies, professional critics, jet-set celebrities and the leaders of various organizations and cults find ways to make the pitch they select heard above others. But everyone is saying to someone, "Get in tune with me."

Parents say it to their children and children say it to their parents. Men say it to their wives and women say it to their husbands. Friends say it to each other. Enemies say it to each other.

Everybody is pleading for Unity. Everyone longs for at least one other person with whom to have that harmony of being perfectly in tune with one another.

In an orchestra, someone is assigned to play the note to which all the musicians tune their instruments. There can be only one true pitch or the orchestra cannot perform.

For all mankind, there is only One True Pitch: God's Truth. We must understand that Truth. God's Truth is not Communist or capitalist, Catholic, Protestant, Jewish, Islamic, Buddhist, Hindu or any other religion or philosophy. All the ideas that separate us are the result of arrogance and the limitations of intellect.

God has no form, so God cannot be male or female, white, yellow, red or black, young or old. All such differences that separate us result from our illusions and from the movies we project based on those illusions. God has no nationality. He is not in a place. And, as a Vibration, God speaks all languages—the languages of human beings as well as the languages of the birds, the fish, the mammals and the reptiles.

That is how each prophet, regardless of the language he spoke or his cultural heritage, heard God's message. The prophet spoke in the language he knew, but his meaning was a result of God's Vibration. The True Prophet and God resonate as One.

The difficulty for most of us is this: We cannot hear God's Vibration until we are in tune with Him; yet we cannot tune our lives to His if we cannot hear the Perfect Pitch resonating within our conscience.

This is why, throughout history, there have been prophets. They resonate with God's Perfect Pitch in a language we can understand.

Why then, since there have been so many prophets, are so many of us deaf to that Vibration?

Perhaps this story will illustrate the nature of our dilemma. A man frequently played with his pet dog by throwing a ball that the dog would chase, grab with her mouth, and return to her owner. If, by chance, the dog lost the ball, she would return to her owner and wait to see if, somehow he still had it. The man would point to the ball and shout, "Over there. Over there." Tail wagging, the dog would watch the man's finger expectantly. The more insistently her owner pointed, the more fascinated the dog became by his hand. As his tone became more urgent and he pointed more vehemently, she became surer still that his finger was the key to where the ball might be.

Our relationship to the prophets may be like that. Each has pointed toward God's Truth. The more powerfully a prophet pointed, the more likely we are to revere that prophet and to create a religion out of our reverence.

Moses tried to show the people of his day how to get in tune with God by bringing them the Ten Commandments. The tablets on which they were supposed to have been carved have become a religious symbol. Replicas of the tablets are placed reverently in almost every synagogue. Yet, have we gone to where those Commandments pointed us? Are we observing those Commandments? Or do we still worship twentieth-century versions of the golden calf such as money, land, power and status, sex and material possessions?

If we became totally obedient to the Ten Commandments Moses brought, we would be in tune with God.

Muhammad tried to show the people of his day how to get in tune with God. He gave the five faruls, or obligations, that, if practiced, would lead to Harmony with Allah. Those faruls are reverently etched in every mosque. Yet, have we gone to where those obligations pointed us? Are we performing those duties? Or have we ignored even the first obligation of charity? Are we charitable even toward members of our own family if they make some mistake that hurts us?

If we performed the five obligations Muhammad brought, we would be in tune with God.

Jesus gave us a single "golden rule": Do unto others as you would have others do unto you. We hang the cross reverently in our churches, on our walls, on our automobile dashboards and around our necks. But do we follow that single rule?

Jesus said, "Turn the other cheek." But we are constantly at battle in our homes, in business, in the streets of our own neighborhoods and in the war zones all over the world.

Few are moving where the prophets have been pointing.

To be in tune with God, we must have the Qualities of God. Only if we have these Qualities, both within our hearts and in our actions, can we experience His Vibration.

The prophets spoke of the Qualities we need through the various commandments. Earlier, we spoke of God's Compassion, God's Love and God's Justice. God's Qualities can be described in thousands of ways. If we look at the way that Power of life performs its duties in the world, the entire universe and everything in it become fingers pointing at God's Qualities.

If we could choose even one of God's Qualities and work diligently to imbibe that Quality and make it an integrated part of our life, that would be enough. Just as the violinist needs a true pitch with which to match only one of his violin's strings, and then is able to tune the rest of his instrument using the tuned string as his reference point, we too can begin the journey by bringing any aspect of our life into Harmony with that Primal Source.

Now the practice of a Divine Quality is not in and of itself a way. One Quality of God is Patience, for example, since for God there is no time. There is nothing for God to be impatient about. There can be no impatience for a Power that extends through all that has been created for all time.

So the mere practice, through discipline, of that Quality of Patience by one who is inherently impatient will not bring that person into any closer Harmony with that Power than will breathing exercises or recitations of certain prayers or mantras. However, if practice is coupled with the utilization of that witness, the fourth level of consciousness known as judgment, then it will be of inestimable worth.

Look at how such practice might operate. Suppose you begin by practicing patience at least outwardly. Inside, you might still be feeling impatient, frustrated, anxious or angry. Yet, for the sake of this experiment, you are going to control any outward manifestation of your inner seething. You are going to force yourself to act with patience and, with your witness, you are going to observe the results.

Look at what such a practice might reveal in a hypothetical situation. Typically, for example, impatience is a result of a conscious or subconscious fear of rejection by someone with whom we have a personal relationship or, perhaps, a relative stranger from whom we need some favor. The impatient person often sets up little tests that the other person must pass. If, through some oversight or because the other person is consciously or subconsciously annoyed at being tested, that other person fails to pass one of these tests, the impatient person feels justified and announces, "See, I knew that would happen." The relative stranger, who might have started out kindly disposed toward the impatient person, might easily become annoyed by what appears to be "pushiness" or manipulation and, therefore, have a change of heart. In short, impatience nearly always antagonizes and causes some backlash.

Impatience usually is aggressive, not assertive. The aggressive act includes the taint of suspicion, annoyance, hostility and other negative emotions. The assertive act is the unemotional appropriate action performed by someone merely carrying out some personal or impersonal duty.

Impatience is always self-defeating in the long run. Patience is always beneficial in the long run.

All this must be observed and understood by your good judgment.

Impatience also may result from your greed, lust or selfishness. It may occur because your arrogance cannot tolerate being delayed or otherwise inconvenienced by another. So the practice of patience in such situations can serve as a mirror in which your witness can see the reflection of your desires and your arrogance.

Impatience may result from an attachment to a religion or a political doctrine that encourages intolerance of those who threaten the security of your beliefs by arguing persuasively on behalf of contradictory beliefs. Your good judgment also must observe this.

Little by little, as patience is practiced, your witness will see and show you all the imperfections that cause your impatience.

More to the point, your witness also will observe and compare the Harmony of Patience with the discord caused by impatience. For, undoubtedly, as you become less hostile and more easygoing through the practice of patience, your fellow beings, who also have fears and anxieties, will find you easier to cooperate with. Some of the stumbling blocks caused by impatience will be removed. More importantly, as you observe the causes of your impatience in that mirror created by your fourth level of consciousness, you will wipe away many of them as automatically as you would wipe away a smudge on your face if you noticed that in a mirror.

If the process were to stop here, however, it would serve no greater purpose than to show you one more way to win friends and influence people. It would not put you in Perfect Harmony with God. There is something far more important to learn through the practice of patience: Obedience to our inner voice.

The practice of patience, initially, fills us with turmoil. We are at war with ourselves, enforcing a pattern of behavior that is contrary to our habitual responses. Over a period of time, good judgment observes enough about the benefits of patience and the difficulties caused by impatience so that a transformation begins to take place. As the outward show of patience gradually becomes genuine Patience, the noise of our inner conflict subsides. And in the quiet, we begin to hear the admonitions of our subtle wisdom.

We discover, for example, that many stumbling blocks are actually warning signs—roadblocks there to protect us and force us to reconsider the direction in which we are going. The detour we are forced to take leads to an encounter that proves fortunate. The ride we were unable to take ended in an accident. In a thousand ways, a very few dramatic, most quite subtle, we discover that there is Guidance in our lives. We see, firsthand, through direct experience, the human version of that inner knowledge that automatically turns a flower toward the sun.

We discover that by correctly observing the "signs" both in the world and in our own conscience, we may be forced to forsake some glitter that would have gratified one of our desires, but we are rewarded, instead, with a clearer picture of the Truth. We develop greater Faith in the existence of that fifth level of consciousness we call subtle wisdom. We begin to experience Grace in our lives. We become more certain that there is indeed a relationship between man and God.

Very rarely will there be "proof" of that Guidance that can be offered as evidence to others. That is of no importance. Each person must experience that Guidance for himself. The "fact" that there is Guidance in your life will not help another person develop Faith that each human being has such Guidance. It is only important that you have absolute Faith that Guidance or subtle wisdom is always present.

That Faith is vital. We cannot always see or understand the reason for every message or warning signal we receive. Sometimes it will seem as though our Guidance is in direct contradiction with what our intellectual reasoning tells us should be the case. We may be tempted to ignore that inner voice and do what seems intellectually correct.

This is a vitally important learning period. It enables us to learn, via lesson after lesson, the difference between "signs" that truly are Divine Guidance and "signs" that simply are new forms of movies projected by mind and desire. This discriminatory capacity must be developed if we are to avoid the fate of those insane fanatics who wage murderous crusades in the Name of God. Asylums are filled with people who claim that God talks to them.

We must use our good judgment to evaluate all our actions—including those inspired by what we believe is that inner voice of subtle wisdom. We must witness the consequences of our actions. Do they enrich and support life as that Power of Creation enriches and supports life? Just as it rains for the weeds as well as for the flowers, will our actions benefit all life? Are our actions free of the prejudices caused by arrogance and the selfish desires caused by illusion?

With Faith in the existence of that Divine Guidance and with the Determination to see and recognize it with our judgment and subtle wisdom, we develop the capacity to realize, instantly, that Vibration that is His Essence and the thought that is a product of mind and desire.

We no longer have to struggle over whether to have Faith in that inner Guidance. We recognize it, without doubt, and we automatically obey it. We obey it because, during this entire learning process, we have seen that, even when the intellect could not understand the reason for the decision made by subtle wisdom, when we obey that True Guidance that emanates from the Essence of God within our hearts, good results. When we ignore or defy that True Guidance, difficulties arise, accidents occur, or some other misfortune takes place.

So just as the outward practice of patience gave birth to inner Patience and inner Patience gave birth to Faith in our own good judgment and subtle wisdom, that Faith gives birth to Trust in God. We see, without the slightest doubt, that it is God's Intention that we should become One with

Him. We see how it is that when we are in tune with Him, the "vibration" of our every action is in unison with His Vibration just as the sound of two perfectly tuned violins will be heard as one sound. We also see that whenever we are not in tune with that Power out of whom life itself comes, there is discord.

We see that whether something gives us temporary joy or temporary sadness doesn't matter. We see that an aspect of that Guidance is that it is the form of God's Intention. We see that whatever happens to us, it is what must happen in order to show us what we have to know to become One with that Universal One.

If we have arrogance, that arrogance will bruise us in some way so that we notice it. If we have attachments, those things to which we are attached will cause us difficulties. Yet, if we have been selflessly performing our duty—without thought of reward or personal benefit—then seemingly miraculous events take place to make our duty easier. If we try to perform that same duty for the sake of praise or reward or in order to earn a good life in the hereafter, we might experience difficulties.

So, little by little, we begin to give up all the goals previously determined by the ego, mind and desire. Little by little, we begin to cut our attachments to things that have form and to ideas, theories, doctrines, religions and other beliefs limited to the level of intellect. Little by little, our Trust in that Divine Guidance becomes total and absolute Trust in God. We turn over all responsibility to God. We surrender our arrogant will to His Divine Will.

We become His instrument. This doesn't mean that we sit, doing nothing until we hear some voice tell us what to do. We perform all our duties as we always did, allowing God to guide our actions. We cannot hammer in a nail without a hammer. But the hammer cannot do the job without our hand to guide it. God has no arms and legs. Whatever our talents and skills, we must use them. We must be the hammer or the screwdriver or the pen or the medicine-giver. We must be in action. But by putting all Trust in God, He guides our actions. He holds the handle.

Only in those actions performed after we have given all responsibility to God, will God's Intention be fully revealed. Only then will we see the Perfection of God; God's Perfect Justice, God's Compassion, God's Love and God's Patience. We see how, even when we forget Him, He never forgets us; even when we blame Him for the difficulties that arise from our own ignorance or selfishness, He continues to guide us toward that state of Perfect Unity with the One.

And in this way, our Trust in Him gives birth to overwhelming gratitude. We see how every knock and bruise that occurs in our lives is in direct proportion to the severity of our mistake, and we say "Thank God," in gratitude for His Perfect Justice. If we receive even as little as a glass of water, we say "Thank God," in gratitude for His Compassion. If difficulties arise, we give praise to God for having created an entire universe that serves as a university in which we learn to reach that realization of Oneness. If Peace and Contentment come, we give praise to God for having provided us with His Wealth.

We see that the true experience of the Plenitude of God's Perfection is not found in some temporary euphoria produced by a drug, a meditation technique, a mantra or by some other trick. God's Plenitude exists within life itself. With every breath we take, we experience that Plenitude. Whatever we have, it is always enough. Life itself is enough.

And as we examine the world through these eyes, we see how His Essence exists as a story within everything in the universe. We see the Limitlessness of God in all of His creations. When we examine our own lives, we see clearly that what is outside is also inside. We see that we are never separate from God.

We see that, though God has no form, no limit or outside that can be touched, we can realize Him through His Qualities. And in that state of gratitude, we become, finally, True Students of God. We realize that God reveals Himself to us through every breath we take and our eyes can study nothing else; our ears can hear nothing else; our tongue can taste nothing else; our voice can speak of nothing else; our every action can serve nothing else.

Once we taste that union with God even for a second, nothing less can truly satisfy us again. Once our vibration and God's Vibration have been heard as One, no other music can soothe us. We long only for that state of union. Thus it is that we become True Students. Thus it is that, just as we began by practicing patience, we now must practice God's Love, God's Compassion, God's Justice and each and every Divine Quality as it is revealed to us moment by moment throughout our lives.

Throughout history, many have pointed toward this path. It is easier to talk about than to do. Our attachments prevent us from acting with God's Qualities. And some attachments may be very difficult to cut.

VIII
Discovering Attachments

Soon after Bawa came to the United States in October, 1971, several of his students got into a discussion about attachments.

One young man challenged another, "If you were suddenly being whisked off to a deserted island and you could take only one thing with you, what would you take?" The second young man answered that he would take only a thin book called Light on the Path that had been an inspiration to him prior to meeting Bawa. The first young man smugly responded, "Well that book is what will keep you from merging with God."

Understandably, the others scoffed and suggested that such a puritanical attitude was farfetched and arrogant. But about a year later, several of the same students were in Ceylon living in Bawa's ashram and they received an unforgettable experience and lesson about attachments.

One of Bawa's Ceylonese disciples had reached a stage in his realization of God that led him to believe that it would be appropriate for him to start his own ashram. After some time, many students were coming to this person to learn about God.

One day, the husband of one of these students came to the ashram in a state of drunken rage. He accused this disciple of Bawa's of sleeping with his wife. The disciple remained calm and tried to explain to the drunken husband that his wife loved only God and that she was a pure and chaste woman; there was no reason to doubt her virtue. In every way, Bawa's disciple showed the enraged husband Compassion and Love. He showed no anger at the husband's insults.

Then, the drunk grabbed the prayer beads the disciple wore around his neck. The beads were a gift from Bawa and the disciple cherished them. The necklace broke and the beads went cascading all over the ashram. The disciple flew into a rage, grabbed the first thing he could find—which happened to be an axe—and beat the drunk over the head.

Fortunately, the disciple didn't kill the man, though the victim had to be hospitalized. The newspaper carried the story the next day.

But at the very time it was happening, some 30 or 40 miles away in his own ashram, Bawa was watching it in a deep stage of meditation. All the young men and women who had come from America were seated around Bawa wondering why he had become so silent. Suddenly, Bawa came out of his meditation and began to describe the entire confrontation. The Americans reacted to the story with great excitement, both because of the grimness of the event itself, and because of their fascination that Bawa could have witnessed something that was taking place miles away. Bawa refused to allow the students to be sidetracked by a fascination with phenomena, however.

"You must have no attachments other than God," he kept telling them. "If you keep an attachment to anything other than God, in one second that attachment can destroy all your good qualities and turn you into Satan."

Indeed, attachments are the chains that bind us to the world of form and nourish the weeds of karma, arrogance and illusion that grow in the world of form. There is no way we can remain Pure and at One with that Formless Power we call God as long as we remain attached to anything.

In a very real sense, attachments are our only prisons. We can never feel trapped if we have no attachments.

Some attachments are easier to see and recognize as attachments, however. (It is always easier to see the attachments others might have than to see our own—even to material objects such as a gift or memento we cherish.) If we have difficulty always recognizing our attachments to material objects, how much more difficult is it for us to realize that we may have attachments to ideas, theories, emotional responses, even habits that most would call virtues.

Most of Bawa's American students, for example, have cut or at least recognized the need for cutting their attachments to icons—religious or worldly. Yet, Bawa had to go to great lengths to cut the attachment one devoted student had developed to Bawa himself. The young man refused to go to work, refused to go to school. He wanted nothing other than the right to sit in the same room with Bawa while he silently recited prayers of love for God. Bawa frequently chased him from the room, but even then, the young man would simply mope around just outside the door waiting for an opportunity to return. If Bawa scolded him for not doing anything useful with his life, the young man cried, promised that he soon would return to work and pleaded for the right to remain with Bawa just a little longer.

Finally, Bawa banished him for a full week from the Fellowship House in Philadelphia where all this was taking place. "At this time, one week from now, you can return,"

Bawa told him. That week was torture for the young devotee. All week he would wait a little distance from the Fellowship for other students who had been with Bawa to come by. Then he would entreat them, "Tell me what Bawa is doing. What did he say this morning? Did he mention me?"

When the week was up and the young man returned, he was told that Bawa had given instructions for him to wait until he was sent for. For hours the student paced back and forth, waiting, waiting. Finally, Bawa called for him and when he entered the room, Bawa motioned for him to come very close and kneel in front of him.

The devotee did as he was told. Bawa put his face very close to the young man's face and, almost bursting with joy, the young man looked lovingly up at Bawa. Then, swiftly, Bawa took the water pistol he had been hiding behind his back and squirted it directly into the devotee's face.

Everyone in the room roared with laughter. Bawa also laughed. The young man, in a mild state of shock, stared from face to face and then to Bawa, trying to understand what was happening.

"I'm just an old man who likes to play tricks," Bawa explained. "But even if your own mother and father were to forget you or neglect you, God never forgets His children even for a second. God is your friend. God is the only friend you can depend on always, forever. The love you have for me, you must have for all of God's creations. That would be very good. But you must cut all attachments. Can you earn a living sitting here staring at me? Can you become a man, get married, support a family? What is the point of sitting here getting water shot in your face? You must have no attachments. God is your friend."

Much later, the student recalled his state at the time this way: "It was as though the water in my face woke me from a deep slumber. The very fact that Bawa would do such a thing was so outrageous that it broke through all my mindsets about him and for the first time I was able to hear what he was telling me about my attachment to him. Suddenly, I realized he had been telling me the same thing for weeks, but this time I was able to hear it."

Obviously, it is important for us to distinguish between Love and attachment. Similarly, we must distinguish between duty and attachment.

Consider, for example, the disciple who, in his late 30s, had worked diligently all his life as both a provider and as a volunteer for various worthwhile causes. Having decided that it was important for him to understand the relationship of the human being and God more fully, he had entered the so-called "path to enlightenment" with much the same kind of zeal and determination that he had been summoning for every other task he undertook.

One day, he came to Bawa deeply perturbed. "Bawa," he began, "you frequently tell us to cut our attachments with the sword of Wisdom. Well, it seems that whatever this thing is that you call Wisdom is trapped inside some other attachment. So I can't use that Wisdom until the attachment that surrounds it is cut. That's why I have come to you for help."

Bawa responded by telling the story which is paraphrased here:

Once there was a young lad who worked to support nine brothers and sisters as well as his mother and father. At 6 a.m., he would milk a neighbor's cow in order to earn a little money. Then he would rush to the train station to see if he could earn a few tips for carrying people's bags. At 9 a.m., he reported for work at his full-time job. At noon, he rushed to a nearby lunch counter to wait on tables. Then he rushed back to his full-time job where he worked until 5 p.m., at which time he rushed back to the train station in order to earn a few more tips.

The boy's family often told him that if it were not for him, they would all starve to death. So each day, he returned home exhausted, turned over his meager earnings, and smiled as he was told, "If it were not for you, we would all die."

One day, as the boy was rushing from one job to another, a guru saw him and recognized in the boy's determination a real potential to see and know God. He tried to stop the boy to talk to him, but the boy rushed past, calling out over his shoulder, "I'm sorry, Swami, but I must keep working. Without me, eleven other people would starve to death."

The next day, the guru waited where he had seen the boy the day before, and as the lad came rushing past, the guru held up a 10-rupee bill. "Would you earn more than this in tips at the train station?" the guru asked. "No," the boy replied. "Then please," said the guru, "take this money and come talk with me."

After just a little conversation, the guru realized how the family had trapped the youngster into believing that he was responsible for their survival. He also saw that the boy now had an attachment to his self-image as his family's savior. So the guru proposed a plan which the boy accepted.

"First we will go and buy enough provisions to last for three days," the guru explained. "We also will buy some material for clothing. Then you take these things home and about an hour after you arrive, take this pill. It will put you into a state in which you will appear to be dead, but you will be able to hear everything that goes on around you. After two days, I will come and give you the antidote that will arouse you."

The boy obediently followed the guru's instructions and,

after he appeared to die, the family began to wail in horror. "Oh, what will we do?" one asked. "We might as well throw ourselves in the well and drown," another answered. "That would be better than starving to death," another agreed. "Yes," still another joined in, "now that he is dead, our situation is hopeless. We will slowly die." "We might as well throw ourselves in the well and get it over with," still another wailed. As they all began to cry at their fate, one suddenly realized, "We still have food. We can wait and kill ourselves after the food runs out."

So for two days, the family gorged on the food and talked about throwing themselves in the well. For two days, they made themselves pretty clothes from the material the boy had brought and cried and cried about how all was hopeless.

Then the guru showed up. "Why all the crying?" he asked. "We are going to starve to death," one responded. "Our brother has died," another explained, "and he was the only one of us to work and bring home money for food." "Yes," another sobbed, "we don't know how to work and now we will all die." "We're going to throw ourselves in the well," the mother wailed. "We're going to drown ourselves and get it over with," the father whined.

"Wait," the guru said. "We can solve this problem. I happen to know the angel of death and he is not such an unreasonable fellow. I can explain to him that if he takes this boy, eleven other people also will die. Since he only wants one life, I can offer him one of you, and he will give this boy back his life. Isn't it better that way? Then only one of you dies, and the boy can go on working to support all the rest." Then the guru turned to the father and said, "You have lived the longest. Why don't I tell the angel of death to take you?"

"No, no, no," the father shrieked. "I can work. I can get

work harvesting tea. This Swami is crazy. There's no reason for me to die."

"Then what about you, mother?" the guru asked. "Swami, you must be really crazy," the mother cried out. "I can take in laundry." "I can earn my living by begging," an older brother protested. "I can work as a seamstress," a sister wailed. And when the guru persisted that one of them should volunteer to take their dead brother's place, one by one, all of them ran away.

When they had vanished, the guru fed the boy the antidote and he sat up. "Did you hear?" the guru asked. "Did you realize what kind of a trap you were in? You were so busy fulfilling your image of yourself as the family's savior, that you never took the time to examine whether or not they could have worked, too. Worse yet, you never took the time to inquire about God, and about who you are, or about what special relationship might exist between a Human Being and God. You were trapped by your attachment to your own image of yourself. Yet, what was it you took so much pride in? Even a donkey is capable of carrying other people's loads. You were born as a Human Being. You must find out what a Human Being is and what your duties are as a Human Being."

Any attachment, whether to a religious ritual, a cherished possession, a role or position in the world, or a self-image, limits the growth of a human being. Remember the example given before of a tree that sprouts in the shade of an older tree. If left alone, that young sapling will begin to grow sideways until it gets its own share of sunlight. Then it will grow upwards, eventually maturing and bearing whatever fruit it was intended to bear. But if, while still a sapling, someone tied it to a straight pole so that it was forced to grow straight, it would become stunted and it might even die prematurely.

Our attachments also stunt our growth; rob us of our true potential as Human Beings. That same Wisdom that is built into the life force of a tree and instructs it on how to grow in order to reach its full potential also exists in a far more sophisticated manner within each human being. If we could untether our lives from the subtle poles to which we are attached, that built-in Wisdom would instruct us.

How can we discover these subtle poles to which we are attached? If you have been fortunate enough to find a True Teacher such as Bawa Muhaiyaddeen, that Teacher will act as a mirror in which those subtle poles that otherwise might seem invisible will be revealed. It also may be possible for you to activate that fourth level of consciousness which we have called judgment.

There is a closed-circuit television system built into the consciousness of human beings. It is as though a TV camera is posed inches above your head filming all your actions and reactions throughout your life. There is a monitor stationed just between your eyebrows. If you watch the playback of this closed-circuit system on your monitor often enough, it eventually will show you your attachments.

However, you cannot argue with the mirror image revealed by the True Teacher or with the built-in monitoring system as though you were still a child arguing with your parents. The pictures you will see were not created by any-one in order to chastise or embarrass you. No one is finding fault with you or judging you but your own good judgment. If you rationalize about what you see or argue in protest, you are only arguing with yourself.

Of course, that habit of justifying our actions to ourselves may be the most difficult attachment to realize of all. Many of us have an attachment to the "big excuse" in one form or another.

The most popular "big excuse" probably is "society." "I'm the way I am because society made me this way." "There's no way to find contentment in this society." "If I lived in the woods without the pressures of society, I could give up drinking in a minute." "I only smoke grass to get my head together after a whole day out there in the world." "If I could get out of this nine-to-five rat-race, then I could really get it together." "I'd love to have a whole year where I didn't have to do anything but meditate."

Often, the "big excuse" is disguised as some version of, "I'm not good enough." Here are a few: "I know I should give up smoking, but I just don't have the will power." "I know I should be saving some of my money, but I just spend it compulsively." "I know I should get to work on time, but I just can't seem to wake up in the morning." "I know I have to lose some weight, but I just can't seem to resist those desserts."

Naturally, people feel that once they admit they are not good enough to do whatever it is their good judgment has shown them needs to be done, they can shuck all further responsibility in the matter. In actuality, however, "I'm not good enough" is about as weak an excuse as blaming everything on society.

Consider this: The average person is not good (strong) enough to do a hundred push-ups. Yet, if a person did as many push-ups as possible each day, little by little his capacity would increase. Eventually, with determined practice, he would be able to perform 100 push-ups. Strength of character is not different from physical strength. The more you exercise it, the stronger it gets.

Thus, if society and "I'm not good enough" are removed from a person's excuse inventory, he may fall back on "I could if I wanted to, but I don't want to," or its interchangeable companion, "I will when I'm ready, but I'm just not ready."

Obviously then, in our times of reflection—of watching our own acts and role-playing on our own closed-circuit television sets—we must spot our attachments and the big excuses we use for keeping our attachments. Then we must examine, honestly, our discontent.

Most people want to turn off that closed-circuit video the moment they even sense that discontent is coming. That's when they hasten to find some distraction so they won't have to face the truth of their unhappiness.

Yet, though it may seem otherwise, the discontent you feel about your own attachments is an aspect of Grace. Discontent is like the song sung by the mother bird to encourage her young to leave the nest and learn to fly.

The things in this changing world to which we become so attached are our nest. With the five mouths of our five senses, we take in all that mother earth has to offer us. So, as we grow, we come to depend upon the nest as the place in which we are nourished and protected.

But as human beings, we also have a sixth sense—the wings we have called "Divine Analytic Wisdom." With these wings of consciousness we can fly beyond the nest; beyond this world of change to a changeless reality. We can fly beyond the illusion of duality to that Universal One. We can fly beyond temporary joy followed by temporary sorrow to a Limitless world of Peace. We can fly beyond frustration, anger, fear, depression and anxiety to a timeless world of Contentment. We can fly beyond the cycle of birth, death, rebirth and death, to the station of Everlasting Life.

This is why we have been given the wings of consciousness. And this is why, one day, we are no longer able to feel content with the nest and we begin to hear our internal song of yearning for completion.

That song is like the song the mother bird sings when, one day, she stops feeding her young and, instead, perches on a tree some distance from the nest and calls out, "Come. Come to me. Use your wings and fly. Fly to me. Come my growing babies. You can fly. You have wings. Come."

Of course, like little birds, we may fear leaving the nest. We may feel it is enough to expand the size of our nest from the size of a community to the size of the entire world. We may try to ignore the call of our discontent and begin re-examining the nest again and again, hoping to continually find new twigs in the nest from which to derive some temporary satisfaction.

Still, if we listen to that inner song, we will respond to it in much the way tiny birds respond to the song sung by the mother bird. Watch a tiny bird learn to fly. It approaches the edge of its nest and steps back many times. All evidence seems to indicate that it cannot fly. But it hears that song. It knows, finally, that it has no choice. It must try. It must leave the nest. So it steps out and flaps its wings furiously. And in spite of its frantic effort, the tiny bird cannot support itself totally. It sinks to the ground. Only after many attempts to lift itself out of its new predicament does the bird finally experience the release of flying. No longer will the bird be confined to its nest. Its world now seems to be limitless.

With that same courage, we must leave our nest—our attachment to anything, even our "I" consciousness. Our discontent is singing to us. Our yearning is calling to us. And we will never gain strength in the wings of that consciousness we call Divine Analytic Wisdom as long as we insist on remaining in the nest.

We must cut that attachment; stand on the edge and jump. Only after we begin to depend upon God to provide that Divine Consciousness and give up depending on the nest will we start to develop the strength to fly. That strength won't mature in a day. It will take time. But it cannot mature at all if we never try.

IX
Determination Transforms

In some Asian countries the water buffalo is used as a beast of burden. It helps to plow the field, it pulls wagons loaded with crops to the market place and toils for its master in still other ways. It cannot be worked in the intense heat of the afternoon sun, however.

The water buffalo has a great deal of fat under its skin, and the afternoon sun in Southern India or Sri Lanka, for example, is so scorching that the water buffalo's fat begins to liquefy and burns the animal excruciatingly. If that occurs, the water buffalo will break away, run to the nearest waterhole and roll in the mud to cool itself. The Compassionate farmer recognizes this tendency in the animal. When the sun begins to get too hot, he takes the water buffalo into the shade of a tree, ties him to the trunk and allows the animal to rest until later in the afternoon when the heat will be less intense.

When we first begin to cut our attachments, we may find ourselves in a predicament much like that of the water buffalo. The mind and desire will endure the heat of self-discipline just so long, and then the need to rebel, run away and roll ourselves in the mud may become irresistible. We may become like the woman on a strict diet who suddenly goes on a binge and eats three ice-cream sundaes.

Without a little Self-Compassion about how to deal with cutting our attachments, without understanding that we must proceed day by day—just the way we might develop the capacity to do 100 push-ups—we could end up rebelling. So, from time to time, we must find the equivalent of a shady tree where mind and desire can be tied up to rest. We cannot allow the mind and desire to wander free, yet it need not be scorched by the overbearing heat of some cruel self-discipline. The wearing of hair shirts is as foolish as rolling in the mud.

How then should we regard the seemingly never ending films of past temporary pleasures played on our consciousness by mind and desire? It is this recall of old memories that some may regard as the taunting of the devil, and it is this that they would try to purge via extremist methods.

Consider such memories this way: When oil oozes up out of the ground and forms a small pool on the surface, if left alone, it eventually dries up and becomes a crust. If you touch the pool with a lit match while it is still wet, a raging fire will start. But after it has dried and become a crust, you can hold a lit match to it and nothing will happen.

Our memories ooze up into our consciousness in much the same way. There is no need to punish ourselves simply because some almost forgotten desire is pushed up into our consciousness by the mind. If we try to suppress such thoughts, then like the water buffalo, we may find ourselves rebelling uncontrollably. Let those thoughts be. Simply respect the danger that is there if we act out our recalled fantasies. Like putting the lit match to oil, we could be starting a fire that will be extremely difficult to contain. However, if simply left alone, such thoughts dry up, lose their potency, and present no more danger to us.

Patience is the shady tree. Faith and Trust in God is the rope with which we can tie up mind and desire. But in that moment of rest, we must listen again to the song of yearning, for it is that yearning that will inspire the Determination that will transform us.

Consider the salmon. It is born in fresh water, swims almost immediately into salt water and spends most of its life there. Then, it must return to fresh water in order to spawn. If we were to remove the salmon from the salt water and immediately drop it into the fresh water, the shock would probably kill it. In spite of how difficult it is for the salmon to swim upstream against the current in order to reach its spawning area, it must go through that experience.

Two things occur as a result of the struggle. First, the transition from salt water to fresh water is gradual. The fish experiences only a little fresh water mixed with the salt, then a little more, and a little more. Next, the supreme effort that is required to swim against the current and to leap over obstacles transforms the fish. It undergoes a biological change.

Vastly more dramatic change takes place in us. If the "I" in us were removed from the "Sea of Illusion" and dropped into the Ocean of Grace, the shock could drive us into madness. Yet, that yearning within us for God calls us to the Ocean of Grace. This is the time—when we are aware of our discontent and feel that yearning—that we must summon our fullest Determination. For that yearning is God's Intention. It is our conscious contact with that Power we call God. If we follow that yearning as the salmon follows its inner call to spawn, it will lead us to the Contentment and Unity we seek.

If we ignore that yearning out of a fear of leaving behind anything that once provided us with some sense of security or temporary satisfaction, we could sever that contact with God. We could weaken the power of that calling. And that could cost us dearly, for that yearning is the most accurate compass possible.

Think about it. How could we yearn for God if there were not already some inner knowledge of what we yearn for? We don't yearn simply for religious descriptions of God. That doesn't quite satisfy. Nor do we really yearn to just remain in the world with which we have become so discontent, in spite of our recalled fantasies. We aren't content with strong philosophical arguments that persuade us intellectually of the existence of God. Nor are we content with the treatises of pragmatists detailing how to use aggression to achieve success in the world.

No ritual or inspirational prayer seems quite enough to satisfy that yearning. No mantra, no tantra, no yoga exercise, no primal scream, nothing less than direct communication with that Power we call God can quench our thirst for more than an illusory moment. That thirst, that yearning, which continues in spite of all the methods we have tried to satisfy it with, is proof that somewhere inside we know God already and will accept no substitute.

But that yearning must be listened to. It must be acted upon. Otherwise, its voice will seem to become weaker as, little by little, we pay less attention to it.

The body knows what it needs for its nourishment. It is not tricked by imitation foods such as vitamin-enriched packaged bread. Yet, if we continue to feed ourselves with imitation foods, eventually we lose the capacity to be conscious of our body's complaints. We almost stop feeling the physical distress caused by an improper diet.

Similarly, the Soul is not nourished by the imitation religions nor by the things in the world we turn into imitation Gods. But eventually, we could lose that capacity to hear the song of our discontent, to hear our Soul's yearning for Union with God.

So like the salmon, we must have a total Determination to swim against the currents of what society calls "normal." We must leap over the obstacles of friends who will want us to remain the same because they are unwilling to transform. If we put forth that unfaltering Determination, then a very miraculous transformation takes place. The composition of the qualities interwoven within the elements of our body will undergo change.

Here is how it occurs. As a result of constantly listening to our discontent and that inner yearning, we develop a conscious and ever-present conscience. And as a result of our own Determined struggle to live according to that conscience—and the recognition of our own tendencies to rebel like water buffalo and roll in the mud—we develop a Compassionate heart. Those two, conscience and Compassion, act as missionaries to convert negative qualities into positive Qualities.

Indeed, the very negative tendencies built into each element of the body become the steppingstones—as they are converted—to reach that transcendent state in which the body truly is no more than the house in which we live. Let's examine the five elements of the body—earth, water, fire, air and ether—one by one; see the negative tendency built into each; the reason for its presence; and how that tendency can be converted to a quality that will serve as a steppingstone.

The earth or solid portion of the body contains the watchdog that barks at every danger, real or imagined. It is the first to experience pain and, therefore, the first to initiate the emotion we experience as fear. Now, it is easy to say that we must be the master of the watchdog and not allow the watchdog to control our lives. In actual practice, however, it is often the harassment of the watchdog's barking that drives men to sacrifice their entire lives to a vain attempt to achieve power and security. They seek wealth, status, power or position in the world as fortresses to protect them from the unnamed fears initiated by their barking dogs.

J. Paul Getty, once recognized as the richest man in the world, was asked why he still worked so hard. His answer: "Well, you know, a million dollars isn't what it used to be."

No one has ever found a way to still the barking of his watchdog via wealth or power. No merchant prince, from the earliest nomadic traders to Howard Hughes, no great warrior, from the earliest tribal chiefs to Adolph Hitler, no power-hungry ruler from the kings of the earliest city-states to Richard Nixon, has ever been free of that harassment.

Only Trust in God controls that built-in watchdog. It still will bark. It should. That is its function. The body needs an alarm system. But the response to the barking must be alertness and Trust in God—not fear. Indeed, fear causes mistakes in judgment (thus the expression "scared out of his wits"). Trust in God allows us to be open to that inner Wisdom that guides us with uncanny Perfection.

Just as the Quality of Patience has to be practiced before it becomes our natural state, Faith must be practiced. It is not easy to maintain Faith in the face of fear. Yet, Compassion for ourselves and the Wisdom within our own conscience must ultimately bring us to realize that fear must be converted to Faith or we will never have True Peace.

Of course, it is difficult to learn to truly Trust God. But at one time, it was hard for us to believe that we could float on the water. Someone, perhaps a parent, pleaded with us to lift our feet up and just lean back on the water. We might have been terrified. Whoever was teaching us to float probably said, "I'll be holding you." But we no doubt whined, "My head will fall in." "You won't fall under. I'll be holding you. I won't let you fall under. Try it. Try it," the teacher probably urged.

Finally, of course, we did trust the teacher. We still didn't trust the water. There was no way we could imagine that something as soft and penetrable as water could hold us up. Yet, little by little, as we experienced the sensation of floating, we no longer needed the parent nearby to hold us. In fact, we probably insisted at some point that we could do it ourselves.

It is infinitely more difficult to learn that God will sustain you. Water you can touch and see. You can only feel God as a yearning or, in the beginning, as your conscience. You can't see God.

Moreover, it is difficult to find a father to "hold you up" while you gradually transform your fear into Faith. Of those who might pretend to be loving fathers willing to teach you the floating technique known as faith, most turn out to be professional, self-seeking businessmen who, not wanting to lose a customer, would never teach you to depend on God. It is in their vested interest to teach you to depend on them, or on their method, or on their church.

So it is not surprising that so few of us have even begun to understand what Trust in God really means. Yet, it can be practiced. And, once practiced, it can be learned as easily as learning to float. All we need to start with is enough Courage and Determination to "lift our feet up and lean back" into it.

Once that process has begun, once our Faith has developed sufficiently enough to call forth evidence of the reality of God in our lives and we can see for ourselves how fear is transformed into Faith, we then can deal with the next task: Transforming the lust inherent in the water or liquid portions of the body into Love for God.

Just as fear, once transformed, becomes the steppingstone called Faith, lust also can be transformed into a steppingstone. And, once again conscience and Compassion are the missionaries needed to accomplish the conversion.

First, let's examine the lust built into the very juices of the body. Just as the demands of fear can cause a person to waste his life in the vain pursuit of security, lust can cause a person to waste his life in the vain pursuit of sensuous satisfaction. And just as we have to learn that the Peace and security we seek only can be found through Trust in God, we must discover that the satisfaction we seek only can be found in the Love of God. So-called free love never succeeded in satiating anyone. Yet, in response to feelings of lust, men have abandoned their wives and women have abandoned their children. The highest virtues of honor, integrity and duty crumble under the weight of lust. What is the reward that lust promises that would cause good people to abandon their own good judgment?

The imagined reward is Unity. At its very best, the moment of sexual climax offers a momentary sense of unity. Self-consciousness, that illusion of the self as a separate, alienated being, vanishes. For a moment, we experience the bliss of two people feeling and experiencing each other as one organism. The pervasive loneliness that subtly permeates the consciousness of the person who sees himself as a separate, solitary individual, finally subsides. For that moment, he experiences unity with another.

Such sexual experiences are rare. Yet, they are the rewards promised that keep lust active. Realistically, however, such rewards are as disappointing as cotton candy. As sweet as it tastes, cotton candy has no substance. It disappears almost immediately, leaving you hungry for something more. Similarly, the sense of separateness returns within moments after the most successful sexual coupling. The person who is cold reaches for the covers. Mutual appreciation may remain, just as the aftertaste of cotton candy remains. But the sense of unity vanishes.

Sex itself is not the issue. Children have a right to enjoy cotton candy. It doesn't dominate their lives. But lust—for sex, cotton candy, or anything else—is a negative or destructive force. It must be converted.

We must discover that just as our abandonment of "self" in the peak moment of love for another human being produced a unity of two, the abandonment of "self" in our Love for God produces a Unity with all of God's creations. We must begin to wonder at the mystery of creation. We must begin to wonder at that single power Source out of which every subatomic particle gets its movement. We must begin to wonder at that Source that provides life for every virus, every plant, every insect and every creature in endless variety. We must stand in awe at that Source out of which endless solar systems emanated. And we must stand in awe at that Source that actively participates in our very lives.

We must become awestruck that this mystery we call God, this Limitless Power that is the creator, the sustainer and the nourisher of everything, everywhere, without limit, also exists as a voice within our hearts, guiding us in each and every detail. Just as God is the voice within a flower that instructs it to face the sun, God is the voice within our own hearts on whom we have come to depend through our practice of Faith. Oh, my God, how we must Love you.

That mystery, that awe and that Love is much too great to contain. Just as the exuberant youth wants to shout his enthusiasm from a rooftop, the Love for God that begins in our hearts must burst forth into Love for every evidence of God. Just as a woman in the ecstasy of her love for a man may love any evidence of that man left behind—even his razor on the sink—the Love for God is experienced with every sunrise; the Love for God is experienced with every view of a bird in flight; the Love for God is experienced with every mouthful of food, with every sip of water and with every breath of air. Finally, one begins to realize he is never separate from God. God is ever present inside and outside. The one calls attention to the other. We always are in Unity with God.

Then there is no loneliness, no separation, no alienation. Then every life evokes our Love for God and our Love for God evokes our Love for every life. And within that Love is the Unity we seek. Yet, even at this stage, that sense of Unity can be destroyed by anger—the negative quality inherent in the element fire.

Just as the form of the body produces fear and the juices of the body produce lust, the very temperature of the body produces anger. The elements are not the cause of the negative qualities; they are the material that fuel those qualities. Thus, when we become angry we say our blood is boiling or that we are burned up or that we fly into a rage—like a raging fire. Indeed, any frustration, petty or large, any adversity, real or imagined, any unprovoked insult, any undeserved punishment, any injustice to ourselves or those we love or any unexplained loss or sacrifice demanded of us might provoke our anger. And in a state of anger, our faith and our Love of God is forgotten.

Now, just as fear became the material we converted to Faith and lust became the material we converted to Love of God, anger must be the material that, through the Wisdom of the conscience and the Grace of Compassion, we convert to Determination. Indeed, only a Determination as intense as our deepest rage can serve as a steppingstone to take us to the next plateau.

Consider the story of the prophet Job, for example. He did not suffer adversity because he had no Faith. Job fully believed in God and was filled with Love for God. So the Determination he needed to maintain his Faith in spite of the unexplained adversities that befell him was enormous.

Of course, we needed Courage and Faith just to Trust God initially. But the amount of Determination needed by the person in fear or in pain to call out to God for help is miniscule compared with the Determination needed by a Job to maintain his Faith.

Yet, unexplained adversities do come into every life. We cannot always know or understand God's Intention. When we can see a reason for whatever sacrifice may be asked of us, it is relatively easy to offer that sacrifice. We feel good serving God or noble serving our fellows. But we are not always offered such an easy, explainable route. Sometimes, like salmon, we must not only swim upstream, but we must leap out of the security of the water (our sense of being Graced by God) in order to hurdle some barrier.

So we must remain conscious of three things. First, we must remember always that if we allow some debris in our path, some obstacle or barrier, to evoke our anger and frustration, then we have lost, at least for the time being, any possibility of making it to that fresh pool of Grace where we can give birth to our own full potential as Human Beings. Only if we summon as much Determination to maintain our Faith as the anger we might have felt will we hurdle each obstacle. Secondly, like Job, we cannot know who is following behind us who might need the example of our Determination to muster his own.

Finally, only if we develop such Determination will we have the capacity to convert the desire that exists within the element air into that constant remembrance of God.

Why do we associate desire with the element air when virtually every one of the billions upon billions of manifestations of creation might at some point inspire desire? First, because the vision of everything we see, the sound of everything we hear and the aroma of everything we smell travels through the air. Next, because we experience desire so often in the chest. Something incredibly beautiful can "take our breath away." When we pine for something, we experience the sensation in our chest. We even become "broken-hearted."

Moreover, the destruction caused by desire can best be understood by examining the way we breathe. When we inhale, we take in oxygen which enriches our blood stream. When we exhale, we expel the carbon dioxide that would otherwise poison our system. If we were to inhale only and not exhale, that poison would kill us.

Similarly, everything we see, hear, touch, taste and smell enriches our consciousness. Our consciousness breathes by ingesting through our senses. Our Love of God is constantly enriched by the wonder of our senses. Our Love of God is constantly enriched by the wonder of His creations as we realize them through our senses. But our consciousness, too, must exhale. If we become attached to our visions or the sounds we hear or the aromas we smell or the feel of the things we touch or the flavors we taste—if we make them desires instead of releasing them—then we poison our consciousness.

Just as our bodies can become oxygen-deprived if we do not exhale the carbon dioxide and inhale fresh oxygen, our consciousness becomes deprived of its awareness of God as a result of our desires. Then, one by one, all that we have gained by our upstream struggle is lost. Any desire we hold onto gradually becomes an attachment. The poison of that attachment gradually erodes our determination so that, when our attachment is threatened, we soon become angry. That anger destroys the unity found in our Love of God, and without that unity, lust returns. And the demands of lust cause us to forsake our very faith, and fear, anxiety and depression return.

So it is imperative to convert desire into that constant remembrance of God. Every time we breathe in with any of our senses we must affirm God. We must receive His presence as the Creator, the Sustainer and the Nourisher of all of life. Then, just as we breathe out, we must remember that only God is God. God is the Power from which all color originates, but God has no color. God is the Power from which all aromas originate, but God has no smell. God is the Power from which all sounds emerge, but God has no sound. All forms, both animate and inanimate, originate from that Power, but God has no form. God is the Power that nourishes our lives. All else is waste. All else must be eliminated, expelled, exhaled.

Still, even at this point of constant remembrance we are not finished. We are not yet "home." We are not yet merged totally and completely with God if we still retain possession of the "self." And a great danger lies in wait for the seeker who has progressed this far yet still has not surrendered the self—that sense of a separate identity. That psychic idea of separateness can persist in subtle form even after we have conquered the negative qualities inherent in earth, water, fire and air. It is the material of ether that produces psychic energy, and that psychic energy fascinates the one who has held on to his idea of separateness even when the glitters of the other elements have lost their power to fascinate.

Indeed, one can become so fascinated by psychic energy that he confuses it with God's Power. And the danger lies in the fact that the person who learns to control psychic energy begins to think he is God. Then he loses all else that he has learned, and he blindly uses this newly discovered energy to try to control that which he could not control with his physical body. Such a person may start out thinking he only will use his psychic energy to heal people. Next, he presumes the right to intervene in another's thinking in order, he says, to heal them mentally. Soon, he also feels the right to use his psychic energy to avenge what he presumes is an injustice. Finally, he is consumed by the madness of his own arrogance and he causes incredible harm to himself and others. Every cult has been formed by someone touched by this madness.

So this ethereal body of psychic energy must be converted to final surrender of the self. We must recognize that this element of ether, which some call our aura or astral body, is as connected to the other elements of the body as the atmosphere is connected to the earth. What occurs to one affects the other. Examine, for example, how the ways in which we pollute the earth also pollute the atmosphere and how the storms and turbulences in the atmosphere reek havoc on the earth. In that same way, the desires, angers, lusts and fears of the physical body also pollute the ethereal body, and the storms and turbulences that take place as a result of the incorrect use of psychic energies reek havoc on the physical body.

The affect that the negative qualities within the physical body have on a person's psychic energy are easily observed. The worried, anxious, fearful person may be conscious of his fear only sometimes. At other times, he may not be consciously afraid of anything. Yet, his nervousness permeates a room so that everyone senses it. Similarly, the angry person may not be consciously angry at anything in particular. Yet his hostility will flow out of him in psychic waves. The greedy, lustful person begins absorbing anything and everything anyone has to offer him even before he lifts a finger.

Similarly, the subtlest idea of self or separateness from God retained on this psychic or ethereal level causes the storms that bring us right back into the negative aspects of all the other elements.

When "I" am here, even subtly, God is not.

Thus, the psychic idea of self must be surrendered to God. No loss occurs due to such a surrender. When light merges with light, there simply is more light. When the rain merges with the ocean, the rain is not lost. As it is needed, it simply will be reabsorbed into the sky and will fall again as rain to nourish the thirsty and still, ultimately, return to the ocean again. After millions upon millions of years of rain, the oceans have not evaporated. Like that, when we surrender our self-will to God's Will, that will is not lost. God simply wills for us what He would will for Himself, and what does God will but that each of His creations reach its own potential.

Thus, as God uses the water of the ocean to nourish all that can become thirsty and with no loss to the ocean, God uses the surrendered will of the Human Being to nourish with His Divine Qualities inherent within the True Human Being. God takes His Divine Love that he has stored in the Ocean of Grace found within the heart of a Human Being and He nourishes life with that Love. God takes His Divine Compassion from the heart of a Human Being and comforts with that. God takes His Divine Justice, His Divine Patience,

His Divine Truth and Light, His recognition that each life is as important as every other life, and God nourishes and sustains His creations with His Qualities.

Yet, as long as man has ego, as long as he has even an idea of self as a separate identity, he interferes with God.

X
To Die Before You Die

Perhaps the most perplexing dilemma we face on this journey is the need, one day, to resolve a seeming paradox. On the one hand, we must have, as Bawa Muhaiyaddeen has put it, "the same Determination we would use to climb a tree if a hungry lion were chasing us." Without such Determination, the transformation we must undergo will be impossible. On the other hand, we must transcend the ego. That illusion of our individuality must die. The "I" must die or we cannot merge with God.

But if I am not Determined, then who is?

It is easy to say that it is the Soul that is Determined. It is God within your own inner heart that yearns for Unity with the Completeness of God. But until the Soul is realized, until the I-consciousness actually subsides so that only the One Consciousness of God exists, this answer remains only a philosophical concept.

At one stage in our search, the philosophical concept can serve as a useful guide. But, like all religions and philosophies, such concepts take us only as far as the limits of intellect. Up to that limit, the ego may be quite willing to cooperate with the requests of our inner yearnings for God. But as our yearning guides us beyond the limits of intellect, the ego begins to feel threatened. In the rarified atmosphere of that level of consciousness we referred to earlier as judgment, and in the still more rarified atmosphere of that subtle wisdom, ego finds less and less on which it can sustain itself. Like a person gasping for breath, ego becomes more and more frantic. And it attempts anything it can to prevent the transition into that sixth level of consciousness we called Divine Analytic Wisdom. For in that stage, no ego—no sense of a separate identity—can exist at all.

So, prior to this final stage, ego makes its last desperate stand. It uses what it has learned from its earlier cooperation with our inner yearning, to act as though it is that inner Wisdom—that inner voice of God. It may even direct us to forsake all desire and live the life of a saint. But even then, its motive is not Unity with the Will of God.

Only two things motivate the ego: The promise of some personal reward or the fear of some personal loss.

In the early stages of our growth, when the ego gladly cooperates with that inner yearning, it is in anticipation of some richer, if subtler, reward. As we begin to use good judgment, and as we see that qualities such as greed, lust, envy, pride and arrogance cause us suffering, the ego again cooperates in order to avoid this subtle personal loss.

But such motives are little different than the motives of the chief executive of a major corporation who recommends a program of corporate responsibility in order to preserve an environment in which profits can continue to roll in. Such chief executives call their programs "enlightened self-interest." And indeed, good behavior, even for selfish motives, certainly seems preferable to the blindly ignorant charge of an elephant in heat—a behavior pattern not uncommon in the two-legged animals with human faces.

Yet, we must be warned by the examples so prevalent throughout history of men who attained power with good intentions, meaning only to use that power for the common good, only to revert, in the end, to one form of fascism or another. True Justice is never served even by the most benevolent despot. Similarly, no matter how small our kingdom, even if we reduce it to the size of our own body, the same danger exists.

If we allow the ego to trick us into believing that is our conscience and we become obedient to the ego, then we ultimately will be ruled by its iron fist. Then, just as power corrupts in the world, the power we give to the ego corrupts our life.

To see this, we need only examine the traditional concepts of heaven and hell. The portrait of heaven and hell painted by many religions directly appeals to the ego. If we do "this," no matter what our sacrifice, our reward will come in an eternal heaven of beautiful music played on harps by heavenly angels, while we bask in warm, golden light, consuming exquisitely sweet fruits and singing of love, joy and contentment. If we do "that," no matter how pleasurable now, we will suffer in an eternal hell of maggots eating our flesh while we burn in a never-ending fire.

Yet, the very people who most fervently believe in this portrait of heaven and hell painted by religion will be the first to insist that only those who practice the rituals of their particular religion will have the right to enter heaven and that all others must suffer eternal damnation. What, other than ego, would cause a person to be so blind to God's Justice that he would say, "Only those who belong to my religion can go to heaven."

Does this mean that the same God who provides rain for

the weeds as well as for the flowers would welcome only Buddhists, or only Jews, or only Hindus, or only Christians, or only Muslims into His Heavenly Bosom? Would this God of Perfect Justice cast more than three billion of the people alive today into an eternal hell simply because they prayed to God in the wrong church?

Has any True Saint ever ministered to people of only one religion?

Yet, as long as ego remains, we will make these artificial distinctions between yours and mine; your way and my way. And as long as such distinctions exist, no matter how well intentioned we may be, we cannot possibly surrender to the Will of God. And if we cannot surrender totally and completely to the Will of God, that Unity we seek will forever escape us. And as long as that Unity escapes us, we never will experience the only True Heaven.

Consider this: Whatever heaven or hell may be, they certainly are not experienced by the flesh. Once life goes out of this body, the elements of the body return to their equivalents in the world. The ether returns to space, the air returns to merge with the air, the fire goes into the temperature of the environment, the water is absorbed into the moisture and the earth is absorbed by the earth and becomes the nutrient for whatever will grow next. The flesh will not experience harp music or maggots.

All that can experience that which is Eternal is that which is Eternal in us. And that which is Eternal in us, that Sacred Place within us which we bury under all our acts and games, is beyond time. Thus, it doesn't have to wait until the body dies to experience heaven or hell. If heaven and hell are Eternal, then they exist for all time—including now. In fact, it is the current imprisonment of our Eternal Soul in this hell of our own making that causes our discontent and our yearning for release into that Unity with God.

The ego, in any disguise, is not our friend. It is our jailer.

The Soul is the son of God, the ray of God's Light, the sixth level of consciousness we call Divine Analytic Wisdom. Whether, due to cultural habit, we think of it as Krishna consciousness (Hinduism), the Schechina or revelation of God (Judaism), the Ruh or Soul/life/Essence given by God (Islam) or as the living Jesus (Christianity), is irrelevant. The fact is that we crucify our true life with the five nails provided by our attachment to the five elements of this temporary body. And the hammer that pounds those five nails firmly in place is the ego.

Until the ego dies in us, until we lose that capacity we have to hammer back those nails of attachment to this temporary self every time our good judgment and Wisdom pry them loose, that resurrection will never take place. We will die without ever having been released from hell.

Now we must understand. This is the world of change. Nothing can be changed in the Eternal. The Eternal is what it is, what it was and what it will always be. Change can only be affected here in this temporal world. Thus, what we build with our life here is what we inherit for eternity.

We will not take our body with us, nor will we take our wealth, or land, or family. So if we are concerned about eternity, then we must be concerned about the state of that which can enter eternity. We must be concerned about what we build for our Soul, the very core or Essence of life. We must liberate the Soul now, while we are alive. We must slay this jailer now, while we still are in the world of change. The "I" must die before the body dies.

If we liberate the Soul now, and that Unity with God takes place now, that is what we will inherit. If we remain tormented by an existence in our ego-imposed prison, then that torment is what we will inherit.

A contemporary storyteller invented a myth to explain this point. He told of a frustrated jazz musician who died suddenly in an accident. Throughout his adult life, the musician was totally devoted to his music and wanted nothing more than to perfect this skill well enough to one day be able to play with some of those musicians he considered the jazz greats. When he left his body, he was greeted by someone who brought him to a place where a number of musicians were performing. He recognized many of the musicians as old-time jazz greats who had passed away. He was told to sit in with the performers and make music with them. "My God, I must be in heaven," the jazz musician thought.

Many hours later, the group was still performing. The musician grew more weary than he had ever been before. Still the group continued to perform. After two or three days, the musician finally cried out in agony, "Please, please, please; can't we take a break?" Only then was he told, "We don't take breaks here. This is hell."

When we want anything other than what the Soul wants, that is our hell. Only if we want only what the Soul wants can we experience heaven, for the Soul wants only what God wants, and only when there is but that single Intention is there Peace and Contentment. As long as more than one intention exists, there will be conflict, discontent, frustration, anger, torment and hell.

This is why we cannot allow our attention to conscience—the voice of the Soul—to be lulled to sleep by the apparent cooperation of the ego. There is a very great difference between the Intention of the conscience and the intention of the ego.

The conscience does not judge us. It does not find fault. It acts more like an electronic homing device that beeps constantly to let us know where home is. It is reminiscent of a game many children play. One hides a small object in a room. Then, another child searches for it, the first calls out, "cold, colder," as the searcher moves away from the hidden object and "warm, warmer, you're getting hot," as the searcher moves toward the hidden object. Our conscience acts in much that way. It is calling us to that release of the Soul that must take place in order for Unity to occur. It neither praises nor blames, but only signals us, automatically, much as our own skin signals whether it is cold or warm.

But the ego judges. It offers praise or blame regularly. This is a trick it learns from early childhood. From infancy through to adulthood and sometimes even after we become adults, there are people pointing fingers at us. Parents, teacher, ministers, employers, wives, husbands, friends—all are likely at one time or another to point the finger of accusation when we have done something we weren't supposed to do or neglected to do something we were supposed to do. Symbolically, people may have pointed a finger at us as a way of commanding us to do their bidding.

Most of us become very adept at slipping out from under the weight of such accusing fingers. We may pretend to be in agreement with the one pointing the finger and then do as we please. We may challenge the one pointing the finger. We may use charm or cleverness to manipulate the person pointing the finger. But whatever technique we may have learned, it becomes an almost instinctive reaction to any accusing finger. At the same time, however, the accusing finger also becomes a habitual condition and when, as adults, others become less likely to point the finger, the ego takes over that task. And this puts us into a double bind. On the one hand, we happily install the ego as the judge in our life, especially if it seems to be driving us toward some imagined perfection. The ego replaces our parents, our teachers and our ministers. It is as important to us as a supreme court judge. We begin to feel as though we must win the approval of the ego in order to attain any success or happiness in life. On the other hand, we use the same rationalizations, pretended agreements, challenges and manipulations to squirm out from under the accusing finger of the ego as we once might have used to squirm out from under the accusing fingers of others.

There can never be an end to conflict in such a state. First, we have installed a corrupt judge to make the decisions; corrupt because that ego never will lead us to that Unity we truly seek. No matter how we plead our case, this corrupt judge will always sentence us to the prison of duality. Next, we cannot even find Peace in our alienated or separate consciousness because that instinctive rebel within us is constantly bribing the jury.

As long as we accuse ourselves, we are forced to defend ourselves. And both the accusation and the defense steal our attention away from the voice of the conscience. We cannot hear our built-in homing device with any clarity as long as we are listening to this ongoing trial.

We actually must train ourselves to listen for that sound of the conscience. In the same way we might hold one ear closed while we try to hear what someone is saying to us over the phone if we are in a noisy room, we must hold our inner ear close to the speaker through which the conscience comes to us and close our ears to the sounds of the accusation/defense conflict.

Where is that speaker? It comes to us through that One Formless Place within us which we have always held Sacred. There is such a Sacred Place in each and every human being. No matter how we may have degraded ourselves at various times in our lives, no matter what cherished values we let go of in order to obtain some desire, there always is One Place deep, deep within every human being that is held Sacred; One Place that we would not spoil or pollute or corrupt. No act is ever performed there. No games are ever played there. It remains, always, as Pure as it was on the day we were born.

When we search for an answer to the question, "Who am I?" ultimately, after we have stripped away all the events in our life and all the acts we have performed and all the disguises we have worn, we realize that this Sacred Place is more who we really are than anything else about us. This Place is the Soul. This Place is where the conscience resides. It is in paying attention to this most personal and most Sacred Place within our own heart that we can hear the conscience. Moreover, it is from this Place that we can appeal to the conscience of others, for the miracle is that there is only One such Place.

When I retreat into myself to that Place beyond all acts, all personality, all learned arts and attributes, all pride and all guilt, and when I come together with myself in that most Sacred Place within me—and when you do the same for yourself—we will find ourselves in the same Place. Your Sacred Place and my Sacred Place and the Sacred Place of each human being is One Place. Thus, no ego can exist there.

Yet, ironically, the ego can be of assistance in our journey to return to the Soul, and thus, to God.

As long as we still see ourselves as separate from God, we cannot meditate on God. Whatever we may think we are meditating upon, we actually are meditating on the ego. When the ego no longer exists, when the Soul is released from under the weight of all our accumulated acts and guilts and achievements, then the Soul merges with God as automatically as light merges with light. Then only God exists and what is there to meditate about?

So when we meditate, we actually are meditating upon ego. Indeed, the ego gives us something to meditate upon. So the function of our meditation must be to strip away the disguises of the ego one by one until nothing is left. In our deepest meditation, what we are doing is looking at the levels of ego and saying, "Not this. Not this. Not this."

Then, when no ego is left at all, we will see God. Until then, all we ever see is our own reflection.

Think of it this way. When we go to look into a store window during that time of day when the angle of the sun causes the glass to reflect, all we see is our own reflection. We cannot see what is on display just on the other side of a pane of clear glass. If we become fascinated with our reflection, then we never will see what is on display. Only if we ignore the reflection, only if, consciously, we say to ourselves, "Not this, not this reflection," and peer penetratingly past the reflection do we begin to discern what is beyond the glass.

This is the way we must meditate. We must recognize each thing we see as another reflection and say, "Not this."

Of course, it is infinitely more difficult to see through the reflections of ego to our Soul than it is to see through a reflecting store window. In the store window analogy, the reflection and the perception of what is beyond the window can coexist and this is how it will seem in early meditations. But to see the Soul there must be no reflection of ego at all. Try, for example, to see the mercury painted onto a glass to create a mirror. Only if our eyes perceive no reflection at all will we see through the glass to the mercury.

Wise men have said that the ego wears 70,000 veils. As long as even a single veil remains, when we go to enter that

Sacred Place of the Soul, we will not be able to find it. Like a person lost in a house of mirrors, each time we go to look for the door, we will find only the reflection of that veil.

This is why we need a guide—a True Guru or Teacher; one who is without the veils of ego and thus can lead us, step by step, along this arduous path.

XI
Who is the Teacher?

This entire universe is God's story. Everything in it is a teacher, or guru. If we observe anything in the world with even a little Wisdom, we will discover the lesson it holds for us.

If we study the ants and reflect on their behavior, how much can we learn about the benefits of cooperative effort and Determination? If we watch a sunrise and reflect on the rotation of the earth, how much can we realize about our own tendencies to turn away from the light and cause our own period of darkness? If we look at the rigidity of one tree and see how one of its branches may have cracked under the weight of snow or the force of the wind, then look at another tree that is whole because it was able to bend under the pressure of the wind or the snow until the snow fell off and the branches returned to their original position, how much can we understand about the need to Trust in God and bend to His Will?

To the man with subtle wisdom, everything is a guru. Our own bodies become the Bible or the Koran which we can study page by page. If we must wash ourselves regularly to rid ourselves of accumulated dirt and the smell of our own waste exuding from us in the form of sweat, how must we also regularly wash away the accumulated trivia collected by the mind and the smell of that which is waste to Wisdom and thus surfaces to our consciousness in the form of desire?

Everything in creation is a parable to the person with Wisdom. But how is that Wisdom to grow?

A small seed may contain the potential for a large tree. And all the fruit that tree will ever bear are contained within that seed. The trees that someday may grow from the seeds within those fruit also are contained as a potential within that seed.

But when that seed first is planted, someone must water it to help it grow. Once it begins to mature and it sends out roots strong enough to struggle through the earth and around rocks to find water for itself, the gardener no longer has to bring water to the tree. But in the beginning, someone must water it.

The potential tree of Wisdom within a human being also is like that. The Original Seed containing the mature human being is implanted within every heart. The fruit we will bear as Human Beings with Wisdom already is there as a potential within us. The Wisdom that may grow in others as a result of the Grace contained within the Qualities of God that blossom in our lives also are contained as a potential within that Original Seed.

But in the beginning, someone must water that seed.

If the noise of our own inner conflicts is so great that we cannot even hear clearly the song of our own inner yearning for God, then someone must play the role of the mother bird who calls to us, pleading with us to leave the prison of our nest and learn to fly with the wings of Wisdom.

If our faith in God is shaky, someone must play the role

of the father who promises to hold us and keep us from going under while we learn to "float," or Trust in God.

Our pain may be so great that we cannot think about anything but ourselves. We may be so filled with the loneliness of separation, that we cannot think of anything but some immediate, if temporary, gratification. We cannot even imagine the bliss found in the Love of God. Then someone must come and expose the wonder of God to us. Someone must come who can fill us with the awe of God's Beauty, God's Justice and God's Perfection until we fall deeply and irrevocably in Love with the Radiance of God.

Our anger over past injustices may be so deeply entrenched, that all we can see are the faults of others. We cannot even begin to summon the Determination needed to discover our own faults and correct those same tendencies in ourselves that provoke our anger when we see them in others. So we need a Wise Teacher who can comfort us and soothe our anger with Love while, simultaneously, he shows us, piece by piece, a true picture of ourselves and motivates us to correct our own faults. He not only must guide us to a true understanding of Justice, but must inspire that Determination in us to become that one who recognizes that each life is as important as his own.

Even at that stage when we have a strong faith and love for God and feel determined to purify ourselves and live always with God's Qualities, there may be times when the world's glitters capture our attention and all that we have understood is forgotten. We may realize that when we remember God and consciously put our entire Trust in Him, that Peacefulness comes. We get what we need, if not what we thought we wanted. Yet, because of the ego and because of the desires that grow out of ego, we still forget to remember.

Then that trial begins in which ego is the accused (the

aspect of self that evokes desire and causes us to forget our Unity with God), ego is the judge (the accuser who insists "I" must be perfect), and ego bribes the jury, thus defending and preserving itself.

More than for any other reason, the help of a truly wise one is needed if we are to remove, one by one, the 70,000 veils worn by ego that separate us from our true potential: Unity with God.

The difficulty ego can cause even for one wholeheartedly on the path—and an aspect of the relationship such a person might have with a True Teacher—can be illustrated by this story told by a man who had been studying with Bawa for about five years.

"It had been my habit," he explained, "to meditate each night before retiring in this way: I would try to gather all my impressions of Bawa into my consciousness—all the explanations he has given us verbally as well as all the subtler lessons he has given us by his example. Then, once I felt that I was holding as much of my total impressions of Bawa as possible in my consciousness, I would begin to ask him whatever questions I had. I suppose I realized that to the extent that there is only One Truth and that True Wisdom, whether it comes from some wise person outside of yourself or from that inner Wisdom built into all human beings, I was really only asking questions of myself. But it was easier to demand answers of that aspect within that could be trusted as Pure and without selfish motive if I consciously held onto a symbol of that Purity. And I used Bawa as that symbol.

"Well, one night, I found myself engaged in a spontaneous and rather surprising conversation with that Bawa I had summoned into my consciousness. I found myself explaining to him that I no longer wanted an intermediary between myself and God. I was expressing my gratitude to him emphatically for enabling me to develop this strong faith that God exists and for helping me to grow in wisdom so that I could now distinguish between right and wrong, truth and falsehood, and so on. But now I wanted to experience God directly. My love and appreciation for Bawa would be eternal, but now it was time for me to go beyond loving God only as a result of experiencing His manifestations. I did not want to know God only through His Qualities as seen in Bawa, myself or anyone else. I wanted to see God.

"Then I seemed to hear Bawa saying, 'Right, it should be like that.' Suddenly, my vision of Bawa disappeared. My awareness of myself in my room in a house on the planet earth in a particular solar system disappeared. All form disappeared. The heavens themselves disappeared. I disappeared. There was no viewer and nothing to be viewed. There was only this infinite space pulsating with light—an Infinite Consciousness pulsating with Formless Power. Yet, it was nothing—nothing that can be described. These are only the words I am using now to describe what happened then.

"I have no idea how long I remained in that state of being everything and nothing. All I can recall with absolute clarity is how I felt as I returned to my normal consciousness. As I gradually became conscious of myself in my room in my house, I also became conscious of two involuntary activities. I became aware that I had been repeating over and over again the words, 'Only God is God. Only God is God.' At the same time, I became aware that I was in a state of abject fear. My heart was pounding as though I had just nearly died. I had the feeling that if I had remained in that formless state for another moment, I might have become insane.

"Only after I gradually regained my composure and began to wonder at what had just occurred did I hear from somewhere inside my own head, 'You still need a guide.'"

As time went on, this student eventually realized that the fear he experienced was produced by the ego, which cannot survive in a state of consciousness in which only One exists. The guide he follows now, is found within himself. He no longer feels the needs to summon a vision of Bawa in order to listen to his own inner voice of God's Truth, nor does he need to set aside a particular time of day for meditation. He engages in what might be called meditation in action. That is, he now identifies with that consciousness of Purity within himself, he sees himself as being the life within that Sacred Place, and from that Sacred Place he watches himself in action. When his actions are not in Harmony with the Purity of his intentions, he modifies them. He accepts this as an ongoing process, like tuning and retuning a violin so that only the correct notes are played.

Indeed, just as a violin will go out of tune from normal use or even as a result of changes in the temperature, the Man of Wisdom must constantly adjust his actions so that they stay in tune with the Perfect Pitch of the Will of God. As long as we express God's Will through these changing bodies, we constantly will be tuning our actions.

The Guide, Teacher, Guru, is needed to teach us how to go inside to hear God's Perfect Pitch, and he is needed to teach us how to tune ourselves to His Will. When that is done, then it is our duty to play God's music via His Qualities so that others will hear and be inspired.

But how do we find such a Teacher? There are so many today who represent themselves as gurus or guides to the promised land of contentment. Some wear the cloth of organized religions. Some form cults of their own design. Some come dressed as scientists with new theories about human origin, destiny and behavior. Some say they have developed miraculous techniques. Some sell you a magic word. Some sell you a weekend of group dynamics.

All of those who have become successful in their businesses know enough to make you feel as though you got something for your time, effort and money. Many, like some in the medical professions, have learned how to relieve the symptoms of your distress even though they cannot offer you the only cure you seek: The realization of God.

With so many people benefiting from our yearning for Truth, how are we to recognize the True Teacher? How are we to recognize the one who has no intention other than God's Intention?

Let us review quickly some of what we already may have understood. When we begin to evaluate our lives with that fourth level of consciousness we called judgment, we also start become conscious of our own duality. "I" act and "I" also judge. To resolve this conflict, little by little we become aware of that fifth level of consciousness we called subtle wisdom. It is that subtle wisdom we depend upon to keep us honest. It is that wisdom that can distinguish between the act and the genuine yearning.

So we install that subtle wisdom as a kind of witness. For a long time, we still identify with the actor, the one who has learned by watching and imitating others, how to function in the world. But we employ the witness to watch our act and inform us whether it is serving a negative or positive purpose.

Then, little by little, we discover that we identify more with the witness and less with the performer. Little by little, we recognize the performer as simply a skilled imitator and that, in truth, we must be something else. Only as we identify more and more with the wisdom who witnesses can that witness surrender itself to the Soul or that sixth level of consciousness we called Divine Analytic Wisdom. Divine

Analytic Wisdom then uses the skilled performer to carry out the Will of God.

All our skills remain intact. But the intention with which they are used will be God's Intention—not the intention of the ego, the mind, the body or desire.

Danger occurs when we have not yet surrendered totally to our Soul. Danger occurs when we identify, even a little, with the performer.

We might become aware of the call to write about God. So we call upon the learned skills of prior performance as a writer. If we still identify with this performer, we may not feel content simply serving as a tool. The "I" learned how to write, so if writing skills are called for, the "I" will try to come along and enjoy some of the credit or applause. The "I" always has some personal (separate) goal.

If the "I" is discarded, then writing skills are a tool in much the way a hammer is a tool or a scissors is a tool. Any talent or skill is no more than a tool.

If we are truly serving God's Will, then the sum-total of who we are becomes a tool for God. We have no vested interest in how it comes out. The pot doesn't taste what it is cooking. As soon as we do have a vested interest, as soon as we preconceive how we think it ought to come out, then the "I" has crept into our consciousness and we have blocked out God.

In the world, everything is an act. The role of father is an act. The role of writer is an act. The role of merchant is an act. And the role of guru also is an act. All the skills we have acquired with which we perform any act are tools. The question is who holds the tools—the performer or God?

If we see it as a duty to be a good father and if we decide in advance what a good father should be and how a child should be raised, then that becomes our intention, and the

"I" or performer holds the tools.

If, instead, that subtle wisdom goes inside and asks, "What is God's Will? What would God have me do?" the answer that will come will be one that serves His Intention and there will be no mistakes committed. By the very Determination to move the "I" out of the way, we open that fountain of Grace that exists within each heart and His answer comes.

God is the only Faultless One.

The True Teacher is not one who encourages his students to spend all their time sitting at his feet. He will not encourage them to ignore their duties in the world and work only for one particular esoteric group. Instead, the True Teacher will explain that we must walk on two legs. We must consider our duty in the world as one leg and our duty to be in Unity with God as the other. Since God is One who performs all duties unselfishly, we cannot be in Unity with God if we shirk from any responsibility in the world. Yet, we cannot do our duty in the world correctly if we go with any intention other than God's. We cannot do our duty to God without doing our duty in the world, and we cannot do our duty in the world without doing our duty to God.

The True Teacher is one who encourages us to walk on both legs. He will not allow us to use him as a crutch.

Thus, when Bawa used the battery charger as an example to illustrate a point about his role, he added, "You need a battery to turn on a flashlight in order to see your way in the dark. You need a battery to turn on your tape recorders in order to hear the sound that has been taped. In the same manner, you need Wisdom in order to see God's Light and in order to hear God's Word. Alright. The Teacher can recharge your battery. If the bulb in your flashlight is loose and no connection is being made, the Teacher can show you how to tighten the bulb. If a wire is loose in the tape recorder, perhaps the Teacher can discover it and help you repair it. If the Teacher is plugged into God, all these things can be done. But the Teacher cannot turn on the switch. The flashlight may be in perfect working order, but if you don't turn on the switch, no light will come. The tape recorder may be operable, but if you don't turn on the switch, no sound will come. The Teacher cannot turn on the switch. You must turn on the switch."

What is the switch? That Trust in God. That absolute Faith that permits you to wrest control of your life away from the ego and turn it over to that presence of God you have discovered within your formless heart.

When you no longer depend for your very survival on some gut-level animal instinct within yourself—when you no longer depend on the knowledge stored in your intellect or on the skills you have acquired; when you no longer depend upon a parent, a teacher, a guru or anyone or anything other than God—then you have turned on the switch.

The moment all fear and doubt leaves you, the moment your personal goals and intentions fade away, the moment there no longer is attachment to the body, to the mind or to any desire, the moment you have let go completely of anything other than God, that switch is on. Then there is only His Light, His Sound, His Vibration, His Power, His Grace, His Beauty, His Compassion, His Love, His Truth, His Justice, His absolute and total Contentment.

Then you see that the Guru is within you. The True Teacher is that Divine Analytic Wisdom, that Soul, that Essence of God. And within that Divine Analytic Wisdom is the total Effulgence of God. And within that Effulgence of God is the Power of God. And within that Power of God is that Original Source. And within that Original Source are all the universes and all the prophets and all the messengers and all the human beings and everything that exists.

There is nothing other than God and only God is.

You cannot come to this realization without a True Teacher. But there is no True Teacher. There is only God. The True Teacher is that one who knows there is only God.

God must be your Teacher. You must put your Trust in God. That inner voice that comes to you and says, "You can let go now and Trust in God," is God's Vibration. It is heard, not with your ears, but by your Soul.

Until that inner voice is revealed to you, it may not be possible for you to become aware of anything other than the "I" in you that can be trusted. If the teacher has not placed his entire Trust in God, he cannot reveal that inner voice to you either. But in a relationship with a Teacher who has surrendered totally to God, you may come to realize that True Teacher within yourself. And that Teacher will lead you to God.

Thus, it is not good enough to choose a teacher on the basis of his act. You must, instead, examine the totality of his surrender to God. Does he keep anything for himself? Does he keep money or give himself comforts that cannot be enjoyed by others? Does he keep pride in his status or position? Whatever he has kept, he has not surrendered that veil of his ego to God. And whatever he has not surrendered, that becomes the chain that binds him to the limits of his own resources—his own learned skills. His resources may be great. He may have learned much. But what is there that is equal to God?

There are teachers today who operate flourishing businesses because they have learned to dazzle potential students with the seeming miracles they can perform. One presses his fingers on your eyeballs, and when you see stars he tells you that is the Light of God. Another makes sweet food appear in his hand, much as a magician might make a deck of cards or a lit cigarette appear "by magic." Still another claims he can float in the air. Scores of teachers solicit paying students by demonstrating an ability to read minds.

These are all acts. They tell us nothing about the performers' intentions. They are side-show events at a circus. Just as discovery of our own psychic energies can distract us from discovering the true miracle of how we exist as One within God and how God exists within us, these magic tricks distract us from the main even—the True Miracle going on in the big tent.

Several American students visiting Bawa in Sri Lanka became fascinated by the stories of Bawa's miraculous feats that have become local legends. Once, when a woman allegedly died while giving birth to a child, she was rushed from the hospital to Bawa's ashram. The story goes that Bawa revived her and helped her deliver her child. Another story has it that Bawa was giving a discourse in one part of the island and simultaneously appeared to a man in another part of the island and delayed that man long enough to help him avoid a fatal accident.

After about a week of such gossip, Bawa summoned all his visitors and lectured, "Do you see a rose? That is a miracle. Who could create that rose other than God? Do you see a tiny ant? That is a miracle. Who could create that miracle other than God? Do you see that tree? Do you see that bird? Do you see yourself? Who could create any life other than God? God is the only Miracle. There is no miracle other than God. Nothing that this old fool does is a miracle. I am a very small one. I am the most discarded of beings. There is no one less important than I. There is no one more insignificant. I am nothing. Only God is worthy of praise. Have eyes only for God. See only God. Only God."

The True Teacher is one who has discarded himself. He has no intention other than God's Intention. He is only the tool.

Another story from the days when American students visited in Sri Lanka may help amplify that point. The students wanted to tape all of Bawa's discourses while they were in that country. But if they recorded using the converter that permitted them to plug into that country's 215-volt electricity, it recorded at the wrong speed. If the tape then was played on machines operated by battery or the 110-volt electricity used in the U.S., Bawa's voice sounded like that of a chipmunk. So the students decided to record only on machines operated by battery. But there were no replacement batteries in Sri Lanka, so they sent to the U.S. for a battery charger.

When Bawa saw the students recharging batteries, he commented, "The True Teacher is like that machine. You come and your wisdom—your batteries—are too weak to turn on that light with which to see God. So you give over the responsibility to the Teacher and he recharges them. But the Teacher is only a machine. Just as the electricity does all the work for those batteries, God does all the work for your wisdom. The Guru is just the machine that is plugged into God."

The True Teacher has no pride. He takes no credit for himself for anything that occurs. He does not even see himself as some extra special tool. He simply stays focused on that Essence which is the Unchanging God within our lives. Thus, he always is listening to God's Guidance. He would perform every duty, from doctoring a child's cut knee to cooking a supper, always staying focused on God; always asking God to guide him.

It is by this example that we learn the Determination we

must have to keep our attention fixed on God every second. Only then will we discover that God is with us and guiding us just as completely when we perform our most mundane duties in the world as when we perform some allegedly noble task.

God does not distinguish between providing food for the insects and the worms and providing food for human beings. God performs all duties with equal Grace. That is how we must perform our duties.

XII
Who is God?

In the early days of American history, many families, hearing stories of beautiful California, may have decided to journey from the East Coast to the West Coast in order to settle in that area. Along the way, to appease their hunger, they might have picked fruit from the trees they saw. Some of the fruit might have been sweet but may not have provided much nourishment. Other fruit might have been sour. If, after journeying a long time, they came to a place where the fruit was both sweet and nourishing, they might have been tempted to settle there. But they would not have pretended that they had arrived at their original destination. They would know they had not settled in California.

When we go to seek God, we may be like those early settlers. Along the way, we hunger for spiritual food. We taste the fruit here and there, rejecting this fruit because it is sour and that fruit because it is doesn't fill us. But then, sometimes, we get tired of the search. We come to a place where the fruit seems tasty and filling, and we settle.

But have we realized our original destination? Have we realized God?

God is not something we experience symbolically. No matter how intensely certain religious symbols touch us or inspire us, God is not a mandala, nor a Siva-lingum, nor a lamp in a synagogue, nor a crucifix, nor a necklace of Islamic prayer beads. If we become dependent upon such symbols for "contact" with God, then we have settled for a God we have to carry with us instead of a God who carries us.

Once there was a boy who was sent to study with a primitive astronomer. The teacher and the student sat under a tree at night and the teacher used the branches of the tree as pointers. He would say, "Do you see the three stars in a row just at the tip of this long branch? This is what you can tell from those stars." Then he would say, "Do you see this forked branch? Follow the left fork about half way out. Do you see the bright star there? This is what you can tell from that star." By using the branches of the tree as a chart, the young boy learned much about using stars for navigation. Finally, his father returned to take the boy home. They got into the father's boat and proceeded to sail across the lake. On the way, a storm came and the boat was turned in every direction. The father, now lost, said to his son, "Well my young astronomer, look at the stars and tell us which way we should sail." The boy stared at the sky for a long time and then began to cry. "I can't tell anything," he wailed. "I need the tree in my teacher's yard."

Once we have experienced God directly, we will not need icons of any sort to point us toward God. We will realize that we never are separate from God.

Indeed, once we realize that we are not separate from God, we no longer will feel the need to pray. What is prayer but the pleading of one who still feels separate and, thus, must appeal to another? In the highest prayer of each religion we plead, not for boons, but for that realization that we already are One with God.

Hindus say, "So Hum"—I am That.

Hebrews say, "Shma Yisroel, Adonoi Elohainu, Adonoi Echod"—Hear, oh Israel, the Lord our God, the Lord is One.

Muslims recite the Zikr (Remembrance): "La Ilaha, ill-allahu"—There is no absolute but for God, only God is God."

Each religion has a prayer to help us remember our Unity with God. But God cannot be remembered with the tongue. A parrot can be taught to recite the Zikr, but it will not realize the meaning of its recitation.

We must not be parrots. We must not settle for simply the inspiration of prayer. We need that inspiration only because we still feel separate from God. We still feel separate from God only because we have not yet lived according to the meaning that is within our prayer.

We must live that meaning. We must know with every fiber of our body, heart and Soul that nothing that changes is real. Only that permanent thing, that Changeless, Eternal Power that we call God, is real.

This world of illusion—change—may be the school, the book through which we can study God; but it is only that Essence, that Power of God that is Everlasting within all that we see, that is God. And that Everlasting Essence within life itself and with which, through Wisdom, we come to identify, is who we really are. We are That. God is One.

"I" am not; only God is.

Other than God, there is nothing.

God is the life within form. God is the Grace within Life. God is all the Divine Qualities of Love, Compassion, Patience, Justice and Perfection within Grace. God is the Power within those Qualities. God is the Source of all creation that is within that Power.

We can see His infinite beauty within those creations.

There is no comparison to God. The "I" must see that. The "I" must look within the heart itself and melt to nothing in its awe of God. That melting must occur. We must look within and without, and we must affirm what we have seen:

Oh God, we have studied the science of ecology and we see the Perfect Balance with which You have created and we stand in awe at Your Perfection. You are the engineer who is beyond all engineers. You are the sculptor who is beyond all sculptors. You are the architect who is beyond all architects. There is no comparison to You.

Oh God, we study the science of human biology and we melt in awe at the mystery of life. You are the Peacemaker who brings Unity to the warring elements. You are the educator who has taught the elements how to transform that which will sustain them into nourishment and how to eliminate that which is waste. Oh God, with what wondrous Compassion You have formed this life. There is no comparison to You.

Oh God, we study space itself and we regard that miracle of creation so vast that there are suns whose light still has not reached the earth after billions of years; and we reflect on an infinity that is but a dot within Your Formless Power, and our arrogance shrivels to nothingness.

And when we become nothing, we discover that what remains is that spark of Your Effulgence that has always been within us; and we go within that spark, that Essence of Your Effulgence, and within that is all the Limitless universes, all the ecology, all the science, all the revelations, all the prophets, all the saints, and that Source Itself.

That Source is within and without. We are within God and God is within us. That which is within and without, that Changeless, Permanent, Omnipotent, Omnipresent, Omniscient One is God.

That is the Truth.

There is no other Truth but God.

There is no reality other than God.

Only God is God.

To realize that, to become that, to disappear into that, so only that Truth exists, that is the remembrance of God.

Until that remembrance comes, until that Unity occurs, we are not Human Beings. We are not True Man. And until we become Human Beings, we will be subject to the hell of our animal existence. We will be subject to the cycle of birth, disease, old age and death; birth, disease, old age and death; birth, disease, old age and death.

That will be our hell. That will be our cataclysm.

People today study what animals in human form have done to the Perfection of God's creation and they warn, as Jeremiah warned, of the destruction that is coming. Cataclysms are coming.

Yet, just as countless billions of individuals have experienced the cataclysm of birth, disease, old age and death, countless societies, countless nations and countless civilizations also have experienced birth, disease, old age and death.

Indeed, in the aeons of life, even the human species may have experienced this same cataclysm. Already, anthropologists have discovered species of man that date back millions of years before the monkeys, the so-called precursors of man. So even scientists now are coming to the conclusion that mankind itself has undergone birth, disease, old age and death.

We cannot say what the outcome will be for this civilization about which only a few thousand years of history have been recorded. But we can say, human beings will survive. God placed within His Original Intention and, thus, within each human being that has been born, the cure for that cycle of birth, disease, old age and death. That cure is the capacity to remember.

God placed into each human being that Owner's Manual for the Human Being—that Divine Luminous Wisdom with which to reach that state of remembrance.

And thank God, He also placed within us that Wisdom of all of the prophets who came to lead us to that state of Perfection in which His Effulgence of Divine Luminous Wisdom could emerge.

God has never abandoned us even for a second. His prophets, His Vibrations, His messengers have always existed within and without. His Essence exists within and without and His story exists within and without. His story exists within and without and His prophets who teach us to read God's story exist within and without. His prophets exist within and without and that Divine Analytic Wisdom, that Perfect Teacher who explains the meaning of the prophets, also exists both within and without.

You must seek that Perfect Teacher in the world and you also must seek that Divine Analytic Wisdom within. That Teacher will show you the meaning of the prophets and the prophets will show you that Complete Effulgence of God, that Divine Luminous Wisdom that is the Owner's Manual for the Human Being, and that Owner's Manual will show you God, and only God will be.

Look at even the briefest explanation of only a few of the prophets with your emerging wisdom. Look with your judgment that has the capacity to see what is changeless and what is illusion. Feed what you see to that subtle wisdom which has the capacity to discard what is illusion and surrender that which is real to Divine Analytic Wisdom. Look both within and without.

Adam represents the form created from the elements. This body we wear is Adam. As long as Adam was in obedience to God, he existed in Paradise. But this body is subject to seduction and Paradise is lost. The body must undergo this exodus from Eden before we feel compelled to look within and see that to which we owe our obedience. Now, we must look within this body and see that which has not changed. See what the Essence is within this body that has been repeated over and over again without change for unknown millions of years. What is that Life that is constant—that cataclysms cannot destroy?

We must examine our life carefully. We must look within the life within Adam and discover that within it is the prophet Abraham. Look within the Abraham who exists both within and without. What is that realization which reveals to Abraham that there is only One God? We must examine that Clarity within the prophet within us which realizes that a statue is not God, that sex is not worthy of worship, that land, wealth and status in the world are not the gods to which we must give our devotion. We first must examine that Faith in just One God that would enable us to sacrifice even our own son to God. Then we must see that when that Faith exists, all we are asked to sacrifice is the goat of our own selfishness. God takes nothing away. God has already given us everything. He has given us Himself and God is all. God is One. Only if we try to keep something separate from God do we experience the pain of separation.

If we understand the meaning of the prophet Abraham, if we look within that Faith with Clarity, we will see the prophet Job; we will see that absolute Certitude; that absolute Conviction. Then no attachments will remain. Then there will be no attachment to blood ties, to land, to public image. We will not keep an attachment to our own flesh. We will have surrendered totally to God's Will. We will have kept nothing, for what more than God is needed?

If we understand the revelation of God that exists within the prophet Job—if we look within that surrender with Clarity—we will see the prophet Noah. We will be able to hear the Guidance of God. We will begin to hear His warning and know what duties must be performed to escape cataclysm. We will understand the Compassion that must be shown to each of God's creations. We will consider each life as important as our own. And in the performance of that duty, in the putting into action each of God's Compassionate Qualities, we will know how to build that ark in which to escape the cycle of birth, disease, old age and death.

And if we understand the meaning of the prophet Noah, if we go within that duty of putting God's Qualities into action, we will see the prophet Moses. We will see that Divine Wisdom which can cut the power of satan. We will develop that Trust in God which will enable us to defeat the forces of evil that exist both within and without. No desire will be greater than God's Power. No magic will be greater than God's Power. No command of the ego will be greater than God's Power. No command of any modern-day Pharaoh will be greater than God's Power. No army will deter us. No ordeal of struggling in a barren desert will frighten us. That Wisdom will overcome all fear, all doubt, all slavery to the forces of this body or the world. That Wisdom will bring us God's Commandments, God's Law and God's Justice. And as we live within that Law and that Justice, we walk with God. All doubt, all fear, all anxiety, all anger and all depression—all concern about anything other than God—will be defeated. That slavery caused by the projections of the mind will be defeated.

And when we understand the meaning of the prophet

Moses, when we look within that Divine Wisdom with Clarity, we will see Jesus. We will see that Ray of His Light, we will see that Soul, that Son of God. And when we examine that Soul, we see the realization of the truth of who man is, who God is, and the inseparable relationship of man and God. We see how it is that man is within God and God is within man. We see how it is that there is only One.

Then we will understand why it is that we must do unto others as we would have others do unto us. We will realize that our hunger is the other's hungry and the hunger of others is our hunger. We will see that if man realized that One Truth, there would be no more deception, no more stealing, no more anger and no more war. There would be only that Perfect Love; that Divine Love of the One.

And if we understand the meaning of Jesus, if we become that Son of God, if we look within that Perfect Love with Clarity, we will see the prophet Muhammad. We will receive that message, that Vibration, that revelation of God's Complete Effulgence. We will experience that Light that was born out of God's realization of Himself in the time before time. We will understand God as God understood God in the time before creation. As God saw Himself, we will see God. We will weep at the brilliance of His message. Our hearts will melt at that beauty. That Effulgence, more brilliant than tens of millions of suns, will burn away every manifestation. Even the attributes of God will disappear into that. Everything will be engulfed in that, absorbed by that Effulgence.

That is why it is said Muhammad is the Messenger and after him there are no other prophets to come. At that state, there is nothing to come or go. There is only God.

That Messenger who must come is not the physical form of the Muhammad who was born 1400 years ago. That form which became manifest at a particular time in the history of mankind is not the Muhammad we must seek. That is not the original Muhammad, the original Messenger.

This Jesus who became manifest 2000 years ago and who was needed at a particular time in history is not the original Jesus, the original Soul.

This Moses we read about in the Bible is not the original Divine Wisdom.

The prophets are the Grace within the Essence of God. Within that Grace is His Effulgence, and within that Effulgence He resides, and all of this He gave to that which would become mankind in the time before time.

God did not give us only His Wisdom or only His Son or only that message of Divine Luminous Wisdom. God gave us Himself.

When we give back that Trust which God entrusted with us; when we entrust God with everything as God entrusted us with everything, then there is only One.

That is the Owner's Manual for the Human Being.

The Owner's Manual is that remembrance.

The remembrance is that La Ilaha, Illallahu.

There is nothing other than God.

It can be very uplifting to recite that remembrance. But if we can say it even one time understanding its meaning, our life would be transformed forever.

Then, before we put a drop of water to our lips, we will think, "Who is it that provided this water? Who is that Creator? Who is that Compassionate, Incomparable One who, even before He created life that could experience thirst, He created this water that would quench the thirst? All praise is to that One. He is that Truth. La Ilaha, Illallahu."

Before we eat a morsel of grain, we will think, "Who is that One who understands the needs of all that has been created? Who is it that created everything that would be needed even before He created that which would need it? Could there be any justice other than His Justice? Could there be any love other than His love? There is only God. La Ilaha, Illallahu."

Before we move a muscle to carry out any intention whatsoever, we will think, "What is this which I feel within me? What is sorrow? What is pain? What is suffering? What is joy? What is pleasure? What is Contentment? What is the purpose of this body that experiences these changes? What is the purpose of this body through which the hell of birth, disease, old age and death are experienced? What is this body made of that it can experience all of this? What are these elements of earth, water, fire, air and ether? What is this war that these elements have with each other? Are all lives housed in forms made of the same five elements? Do they also suffer? Do they also experience birth, disease, old age and death? What is the cure for this cataclysmic cycle? Will the cure for each human being be the same? If I seek a cure for my suffering that is separate from that One cure through which all human beings can end that cycle, will it be a cure? Or will it cause more suffering?"

If we think in that way before we move a muscle to carry out any intention, then we will remember that the only cure is God. God is the only One who has no beginning and no end. God is the only One who has no birth, no disease, no old age and no death. Everything changes other than God and nothing that changes remains true. There is no Truth other than God. Only God is Truth.

If, with every breath we exhale, we also exhale all the arrogance of the "I," all the illusion of separateness that causes selfishness; if, with every breath we exhale, we also exhale our attachment to self; if we say La Ilaha with the understanding of our entire being, then we will know I am not.

Then with every breath we inhale, we must affirm God as the Source of life. We must affirm His Compassionate Qualities within this life and His Grace within those Qualities, and His Power within that Grace and God Himself within His Power. We will fill this house with His life-sustaining Essence and we will say, "Illallahu, there is only You, God."

That remembrance must become as automatic as breathing. Then man will become God and God will become man. There is only One.

May that yearning that brought you to read this book become True Faith. May this True Faith lead you to that encounter with His Vibration which will give you an experience of His taste. May the experience of the taste of God within your life give birth in you to the absolute Certitude and Conviction needed to go on the True Path. May the exercise of the True Path—putting the Divine Qualities into action and negating the influences of the body, mind and desire—enable you to develop that unwavering Determination. May that Determination take you through the examination of each and every aspect of your life so that your discrimination can develop. May that judgment and subtle wisdom that discards all that changes and keeps only that which is changeless grow. And may that subtle wisdom nourish that Original Seed that is within you. May the Divine Analytic Wisdom, that Perfect Teacher that is within the Original Seed, explain to you the Message of God's gift to man. And may that Divine Analytic Wisdom surrender everything to Divine Luminous Wisdom. May everything be absorbed into that Effulgence and may that Effulgence be absorbed into its Source.

May your life, the Light that is the Source of that life and God who is the Source of that Light be One.

This is our constant prayer.
May it be so, oh God, may it be so. Amen.

XIII
Eight Radio Commentaries

INTRODUCTION BY SONIA GILBERT

THERE WAS A TIME in the nineteen seventies when a resonant baritone voice could be heard for three minutes, four times a day on Philadelphia's radio station WDAS, speaking words of wisdom to the listeners. So compelling was the vibration within the messages that people waited in anticipation for them. It was reported that people working in stores or gas stations, people in prisons or in autos became silent, not wanting to miss a word of Mitch Gilbert's message.

Several of those commentaries are being published in this book to provide a taste of something that was unique and very much appreciated by all those who heard them.

FRIDAY, DECEMBER 9, 1977

Yesterday we commented that it is possible to teach a parrot how to recite a prayer, but that doesn't mean the parrot is praying. Now if the parrot is saying the same words we might say, why isn't the parrot praying too? Because the parrot has no true understanding of what it is saying. Therefore, if we wish to pray, we must understand our prayers. If we say, "Oh God, the Most Merciful," we must understand who God is, and what the Quality of that Mercy is. Even then, it is not enough simply to praise God. If God truly is that Power that is the One Source of everything that exists, does God need our praise? Is God something that would have vanity and hunger for our compliments? Is God like an insecure woman who needs to be told she is beautiful or an insecure man who needs to be told he is handsome? No, God is not like that. What God needs from us is for us to perform our duty. Just as the rain must bring moisture, and the sun must bring warmth, and the earth must produce the food that nourishes life, mankind too has its duty to perform. The duty of water is to quench the thirst of every life form that can absorb moisture. The power to quench thirst is given to the water by that Creator. The duty of water, therefore, is to carry out God's Intention. So we must examine ourselves and see what our duty is. We must examine how it is we were created. It is said that God created man in His own image. That does not mean that there is a God somewhere with arms and legs. It means that just as that One Source gave to water the quality that would quench thirst, he gave to man His own Qualities so that we could quench the thirst for Compassion, Love and Justice. That is our duty, and when we perform that duty, we are in prayer. This is Mitch Gilbert saying Truth is the only lasting joy.

Wednesday, December 7, 1977

We've been talking about learning to distinguish between the true revelation that is possible to anyone with a strong enough Love and awe of that Ineffable Power that is the Source of all life and that we call God, and those thoughts and ideas that are produced by our own minds and may come disguised as revelation. A young woman recently told me a story that may help. She explained that when she was pregnant with her first child she went into what she thought was labor a full week before the baby was actually born. Of course, it was false labor. And as she put it, "When I finally went into True Labor, I knew it. There wasn't any room for doubt. But not knowing what True Labor was until I experienced it, I called whatever it was I experienced a week earlier labor." Wisdom, or a true calling from God, works much the same way. When truly Divine Wisdom is operating, you no more have to think about it than a woman has to think about labor. You simply respond—without thought or regard to any reward or benefit that might come to you or yours. You feel that Truth in you in a total and consuming rush. Yet, before that occurs, you may experience other tremors of realization and those realizations may be important. But consider this: True Labor concludes with a birth. And True Wisdom results in the blossoming or bearing of some life-fulfilling or life-sustaining action. If you have realization after realization, yet you continue in the same old way, committing the same old mistakes, experiencing the same old angers, fears and depressions, then such realizations are like false labor. Be patient a little longer. With enough Faith and Determination, True Wisdom will come. This is Mitch Gilbert saying Truth is the only lasting joy.

MONDAY, DECEMBER 5, 1977

Over and over in these commentaries we refer to something within the human being that we label with such names as: The inner Voice, Divine Wisdom, an inner compass or radar system that can guide us and keep us in Harmony with that Power that is the Source of life and that we call God. Recently we said that a man's conscience is the voice of that inner Wisdom, the translator, if you will, that puts into understandable language what is actually more a silent Vibration than anything we can see or hear. And over and over again, these commentaries urge people to be obedient to those signals that come from that inner Voice. There is always a danger in that, and it is necessary to speak about that danger as well. Let's face it, many horrible crimes against humanity have been committed by people who were certain they were listening to and obeying the Voice of God. Throughout history, people have slaughtered in the Name of God. Throughout history self-appointed spokesmen for what they claimed was the Will of God have persecuted, exploited, plundered and tortured and murdered their fellow human beings. Even today, mad men murder prostitutes for God, kill communists for Christ, justify racism with quotations from the Bible and in so many other ways deny human beings justice in the Name of the Lord. So it is important that we learn to distinguish between those voices conjured up by our own minds and the arrogance of our egos and the true revelation that can be possible in each human being. We must be able to evaluate our own thoughts the way a jeweler assays for gold. We must have an acid that will burn away anything that is not the Truth, the way the jeweler's acid burns away anything that isn't gold. And we'll talk about that tomorrow. This is Mitch Gilbert saying Truth is the only lasting joy.

Wednesday, November 30, 1977

Yesterday we were saying that when we learn to live our lives by keeping our emotions in balance just as a dirt bike-rider keeps his physical balance while riding an obstacle course, then living itself becomes our greatest adventure. It's a full-time excitement, and no other form of high or commercial entertainment could possibly compare to it. But most of us, sadly, have very little experience at keeping our balance emotionally. No one taught us, as kids, how to ride a two-wheeler with training wheels, so now, as adults, in a fast paced world that is one giant obstacle course, we just haven't learned to control our emotions the way a dirt bike-rider controls his bike. We don't know how to flow with the turns or keep ourselves headed in the right direction when some surprise bump in life throws us momentarily. So let's talk about that. We mentioned the other day that there is a mechanism in the middle ear that helps keep us balanced physically. We also have a mechanism that helps keep us balanced emotionally. It is a built-in Wisdom, an inner voice that is aware of the Eternal Truth as the middle ear is aware of physical balance. It is not pulled off center by fear of pain or lust for pleasure. It knows that all joy and sorrow, pleasure and pain, are temporary. So, just as the middle ear sends its signal to where balance is in the brain, and the brain sends signals to all your muscles so you aren't thrown by physical bumps or turns, the witness knows where Eternal Truth is and sends signals to your conscience which in turn signals your sense of judgment so that you are not thrown by the emotional twists and turns of your life. If we were as concerned about not falling emotionally as we are with not falling physically, we would learn to respond to those silent instructions. We'll talk about that tomorrow. This is Mitch Gilbert saying Truth is the only lasting joy.

Monday, December 12, 1977

Last week, we finished off by suggesting that most of us are like spiritual primitives. That is, we have little understanding of what our true potential as Human Beings might be. So naturally, not understanding that which we inherited as human beings, we think that any truly wise and holy person is a kind of miracle—something that just happened as a result of some random, magic touch of God. We may worship that holy person, but it doesn't occur to us that the very same potential might exist in every human being. Consider just how it is that man has been created. Every mineral, every element that exists anywhere in the universe also exists within the body of the human being. There is nothing that exists in this world that we couldn't know about just by examining ourselves. When we are conceived and we gestate through pregnancy and finally are born, we go through the entire history of life from the smallest sperm, to the tadpole to the mammal to the human being. We already have experienced more than 200 million years of the history of life. Recorded right within life itself is all the history and all the wisdom of the entire experience of life on this world. We have within us the capacity to know the nature of every animal and of every saint. All of that is recorded within us. And the Essence of that Power from which all life comes—the Essence of God—is also within us. That is who a Human Being is. Our consciousness, if we don't limit it to what we have recorded in our brain, is as Limitless as its Creator. If we limit it, if we say that all we can know is what the five senses have seen, heard, smelled, touched and tasted and then recorded in the brain, then we remain spiritual primitives. But that limit is self imposed. The various prophets who have come obviously threw off the shackles of such limits. We'll talk about that tomorrow. This is Mitch Gilbert saying Truth is the only lasting joy.

FRIDAY, DECEMBER 30, 1977

Yesterday we were saying that the conscience is like a mirror that catches the Light of the Truth and reflects it so that it gets our attention—in much the same way that a hand-held mirror can be used to reflect the light of the sun. You've seen movies (or perhaps you've even tried it as a youngster yourself) in which a person catches another person's attention by reflecting the light of the sun with a mirror, and that's how our conscience catches our conscious attention. I used to think that the conscience was simply that conditioned reflex that occurs as a result of a parent drilling the rules of right and wrong into a child's head. But no one has to ever tell us the things that our conscience tells us automatically. We know, whether anyone tells us or not, the difference between being loved and being treated with hostility. Therefore, we know the difference between being loving toward someone, and being spiteful and hostile. Our conscience tells us. We know, without anyone outside of us explaining it, the difference between Justice and prejudice. We know the difference between Compassion and selfishness, Patience and impatience, Tolerance towards mistakes and intolerance, Willingness to help another and cold indifference. In short, we always know the difference between the One Truth which is supportive of life, and anything else that is even the slightest way destructive of life. And it is the conscience that reflects that Truth. So no matter how much emotional tension or old habits might have pulled us off center, we can still find our way out of any emotional jungle by following our conscience. We know what hurts us and that it must be wrong because it is the opposite of Truth. Therefore, we know that we cannot cause that same hurt to others. That's the Golden Rule. That's the conscience. That's the Truth. This is Mitch Gilbert saying Truth is the only lasting joy.

THURSDAY, DECEMBER 29, 1977

For a few days we've been talking about the ways people go through life in a series of emotional circles, repeating similar kinds of emotional pitfalls over and over again. And yesterday we said that there is a Truth that can serve as a beacon or a compass that can help us find the direction we need to move in so that we can stop repeating our emotional patterns. The problem is, how do you know what the Truth is? It's difficult to find Truth in the world. After all, it isn't just advertisers and politicians who lie. We have to assume that anyone who has some kind of vested interest in us—anyone who stands to gain something from us, even appreciation, or lose something, even just our respect—may be bending the Truth a little, or misleading us in some way. People tell each other little while lies for such reasons, and rip each other off for such reasons. In any event, you can't expect to find the Truth by looking for it from others. But we don't have to find the Truth outside. It already exists inside. We can't see it, or hear it, or taste it, feel it, or smell it because the Truth is a Limitless thing—it has no boundaries and it exists everywhere, within every heart. But we do have something within us that we can hear, that we are aware of, and that is like a mirror that reflects that Truth the way a hand held mirror can reflect and intensify the sun. Some people call that mirror—that device inside us that reflects the Light of the Truth—a conscience. Now we may not be used to listening to our consciences, and we'll talk about that some more tomorrow, but we all have one. And it is that built-in compass that we can use to find our way out of even the worst emotional jungle. This is Mitch Gilbert saying Truth is the only lasting joy.

MONDAY, SEPTEMBER 12, 1977

One Sunday evening several years ago, a number of people showed up at the Fellowship House, where my teacher Bawa Muhaiyaddeen was, and they wanted to ask questions about almost everything except God and the relationship between God and man. They asked him about their jobs, their health, their marital problems, concerns they had about their children; but they did not ask him about Truth. They did not ask him about God. When the morning had passed, and Bawa had answered all their questions and sent them to have lunch, he turned to one of the regulars and said, "I did not travel 13,000 miles to come to America to be a fortune teller. I came to teach about God. From now on, when people want their fortunes told, you answer them." The girl who Bawa addressed this way was flabbergasted. "I don't know how to do that," she protested. "Oh, it's easy," Bawa said, "just read their reels and tell them what it says." "How can I read their reels?" she asked, still perplexed. "Oh, I guess you are still too busy reading your own reels," Bawa answered. "When you have gotten rid of your own reels then you will be able to see the other person's reels." And it's true that most of us are so busy paying attention to what's going on in our own heads, that we fail to see what's perfectly obvious to someone without that self-centered focus and distraction. It's a little like the thing we talked about a week or so ago. We can't see the mirror because we are too busy looking at our own reflection. We'll talk more about this tomorrow. This is Mitch Gilbert saying Truth is the only lasting joy.

XIV
A LETTER FROM PRISON

It was Mitchell Gilbert's remarkable ability to completely absorb the words of M. R. Bawa Muhaiyaddeen's discourses and to then present them as points of wisdom thoroughly understandable to people thirsty for this knowledge. People everywhere have written and spoken of their gratitude. This letter from Diano Bevens is an example of how much this book means to those who might never have come to know what is their birthright. Ameen.

—Sonia Gilbert

God Thank You!

An Owner's Manual for the Human Being has led me to the truth; the inner heart: the Soul. Now that I'm aware and conscious of the Soul, what its function and I must follow the conscience that links us to God radiating Effulgence.

I been searching for this knowledge for a long time: the truth. I know deep in my heart the teachings of this book are true. Thru my experience and what I feel illuminating from my Soul this is the path. The World philosophies and religions confused me, my intellect had me traveling on the wrong path, most of the time I forsake my own conscience. Now I know I'm on the right path because of the enlightenment of this book which gave me faith courage and strength to continue to strive in the way of truth and in wisdom for growth.

I would like to attain the book catalog and if possible send me a copy of *An Owner's Manual for the Human Being*. Also I would like to receive Bawa Muhaiyaddeen address so I can write him. My Soul will teach me many things of God, but to have a teacher such as Bawa Muhaiyaddeen will truly be a blessing.

I'll be looking forward to hear from your Fellowship Press soon. Thank You!

Deepest Respect,
Diano

It's time to be born again,
I've been dieing so long,
Time to wake up and see the rest of the song
Time to hear music from beyond the spheres
Time to know wisdom unheard by the ears.
It's time to be born again,
Give up my fears
Time to wake up from this torment of tears
Time to hear justice instead of desire
Time to make quiet the anger of fire,
It's time to be born again,
Come up from mind's mire
Time to wake up from both lower and higher
Time to hear one note that unifies all
Time to be He, the One who is All
It's time to be born again,
I've been dieing so long.

–Mitchell Gilbert
1980

ONE LIGHT PRESS
Merion Station, PA 19066

To purchase this book,
and other books by M. R. Bawa Muhaiyaddeen,

email: info@bmf.org

or call: 215-879-6300